AUGSBURG SERMONS

SERMONS FOR THE
28 LESSER FESTIVALS
ON TEXTS FROM
THE NEW LECTIONARY
AND CALENDAR

augsburg sermons

LESSER FESTIVALS

AUGSBURG PUBLISHING HOUSE
MINNEAPOLIS, MINNESOTA

AUGSBURG SERMONS—LESSER FESTIVALS

Copyright © 1977 Augsburg Publishing House

Library of Congress Catalog Card No. 77-72465

International Standard Book No. 0-8066-1582-6

All rights reserved. No part of this book may be used or reproduced in any manner whatsoever without written permission except in the case of brief quotations embodied in critical articles and reviews. For information address Augsburg Publishing House, 426 South Fifth Street, Minneapolis, Minnesota 55415.

Scripture quotations unless otherwise noted are from the Revised Standard Version of the Bible, copyright 1946, 1952, and 1971 by the Division of Christian Education of the National Council of Churches.

MANUFACTURED IN THE UNITED STATES OF AMERICA

Contents

Introduction   9

ST. ANDREW, APOSTLE — November 30
He Never Came Empty-Handed
John 1:35-42   Robert W. Stackel   13

ST. THOMAS, APOSTLE — December 21
Faith in God Is Not Enough
John 14:1-7   Herbert F. Lindemann   18

ST. STEPHEN, DEACON AND MARTYR — December 26
Rejected Love
Matthew 23:34-39   Lawrence R. Likness   23

ST. JOHN, APOSTLE AND EVANGELIST — December 27
Meet the Fisherman Theologian
John 21:20-25   Reynold N. Johnson   27

THE HOLY INNOCENTS, MARTYRS — December 28
The Terrible Questions
Matthew 2:13-18   Frederick J. Gaiser   32

THE NAME OF JESUS — January 1
He Has Given You His Name
Luke 2:21   Alton F. Wedel   37

THE CONFESSION OF ST. PETER — January 18
Faith's Rock Festival
Matthew 16:13-19   Mons Teig   40

THE CONVERSION OF ST. PAUL — January 25
The Dynamics of Conversion
Acts 9:1-22   Harry N. Huxhold   44

THE PRESENTATION OF OUR LORD — February 2
Turtledoves, Pigeons, and the Plan of God
Luke 2:22-40   Carl A. Volz   49

ST. MATTHIAS, APOSTLE — February 24
An Almost Anonymous Apostle
Acts 1:15-26   George M. Bass   53

THE ANNUNCIATION OF OUR LORD — March 25
The God Who Would Be Man
Luke 1:26-38   Clifford J. Swanson   58

ST. MARK, EVANGELIST — April 25
Second-string Saints
Mark 1:1-15   Paul W. Egertson   63

ST. PHILIP AND ST. JAMES, APOSTLES — May 1
An Even Greater Presence
John 14:8-14   Frank C. Senn   68

THE VISITATION — May 31
Spirited Courtesy
Luke 1:39-47   Kenneth F. Korby   73

ST. BARNABAS, APOSTLE — June 11
A Great Christian
Acts 11:19-30; 13:1-3   W. A. Poovey   78

THE NATIVITY OF ST. JOHN THE BAPTIZER — June 24
Lasting Midsummer Joys
Luke 1:57-67 (68-80)   Wilton Bergstrand   83

ST. PETER AND ST. PAUL, APOSTLES — June 29
Caught in the Embrace
1 Corinthians 3:16-23   Paul K. Peterson 88

ST. MARY MAGDALENE — July 22
Come—See—Hear—Tell
John 20:1-2, 11-18   C. Richard Evenson 93

ST. JAMES THE ELDER, APOSTLE — July 25
You're the Greatest!
Mark 10:35-45   Michael L. Sherer   97

MARY, MOTHER OF OUR LORD — August 15
Flowers for the Ossuary
Luke 1:46-55   Gordon Lathrop 101

ST. BARTHOLOMEW, APOSTLE — August 24
Who Follows in His Train?
John 1:43-51   Larry A. Hoffsis 106

HOLY CROSS DAY — September 14
Cross Your Heart
John 12:20-33   George W. Hoyer 110

ST. MATTHEW, APOSTLE AND EVANGELIST — September 21
Transformed by Love
Matthew 9:9-13   Charles R. Anders 113

ST. MICHAEL AND ALL ANGELS — September 29
Our Guardian Angels
Revelation 12:7-12   Louis Nuechterlein 117

ST. LUKE, EVANGELIST — October 18
Caring for the Middlescent
Luke 1:1-4; 24:44-53   Lowell J. Timm 122

ST. SIMON AND ST. JUDE, APOSTLES — October 28
Peace Is an Aggressive Word
John 14:21-27   Hubert Beck 128

REFORMATION DAY — October 31
Luther Never Changed His Name
John 8:31-36   Hugh George Anderson 133

ALL SAINTS' DAY — November 1
Blessed Are Those Who Mourn
Matthew 5:1-12   Charles Trexler 137

Introduction

It is also taught among us that saints should be kept in remembrance so that our faith may be strengthened when we see what grace they received and how they were sustained by faith. Moreover, their good works are to be an example for us, each of us in his own calling.

(The Augsburg Confession, Art. XXI)

With these words the Reformers encourage us to include in our worship the remembrance of that rich assortment of persons —young and old, learned and ignorant, people of action and hermits—whose sole common denominator is that the grace of God worked mightily within them. In certain remarkable ways, the people listed in this volume of sermons have shown the world something of the greatness of the grace of God revealed in Jesus Christ.

Many churches, however, have allowed these great examples of faith to go unnoticed. Therefore the Calendar and Lectionary recently introduced by the Inter-Lutheran Commission on Worship (ILCW) has included 28 Lesser Festivals to encourage congregations to remember in their worship services these important events in Christian history.

Although many of these days were included in the calendar and propers provided in previous hymnals such as the Service Book and Hymnal of 1958, the new Lutheran Book of Worship of 1978 contains all 28. Among the most significant additions to the list of lesser festivals are St. Barnabas, Apostle (June 11), Mary, Mother of Our Lord (August 15), and Holy Cross Day (September 14).

Sermons in this volume have been prepared by pastors of the American Lutheran Church, The Lutheran Church in America, The Lutheran Church—Missouri Synod, and the Evangelical Lutheran Church of Canada. The sermons are offered as a resource for pastors and congregations for use in celebration of the Lesser Festivals.

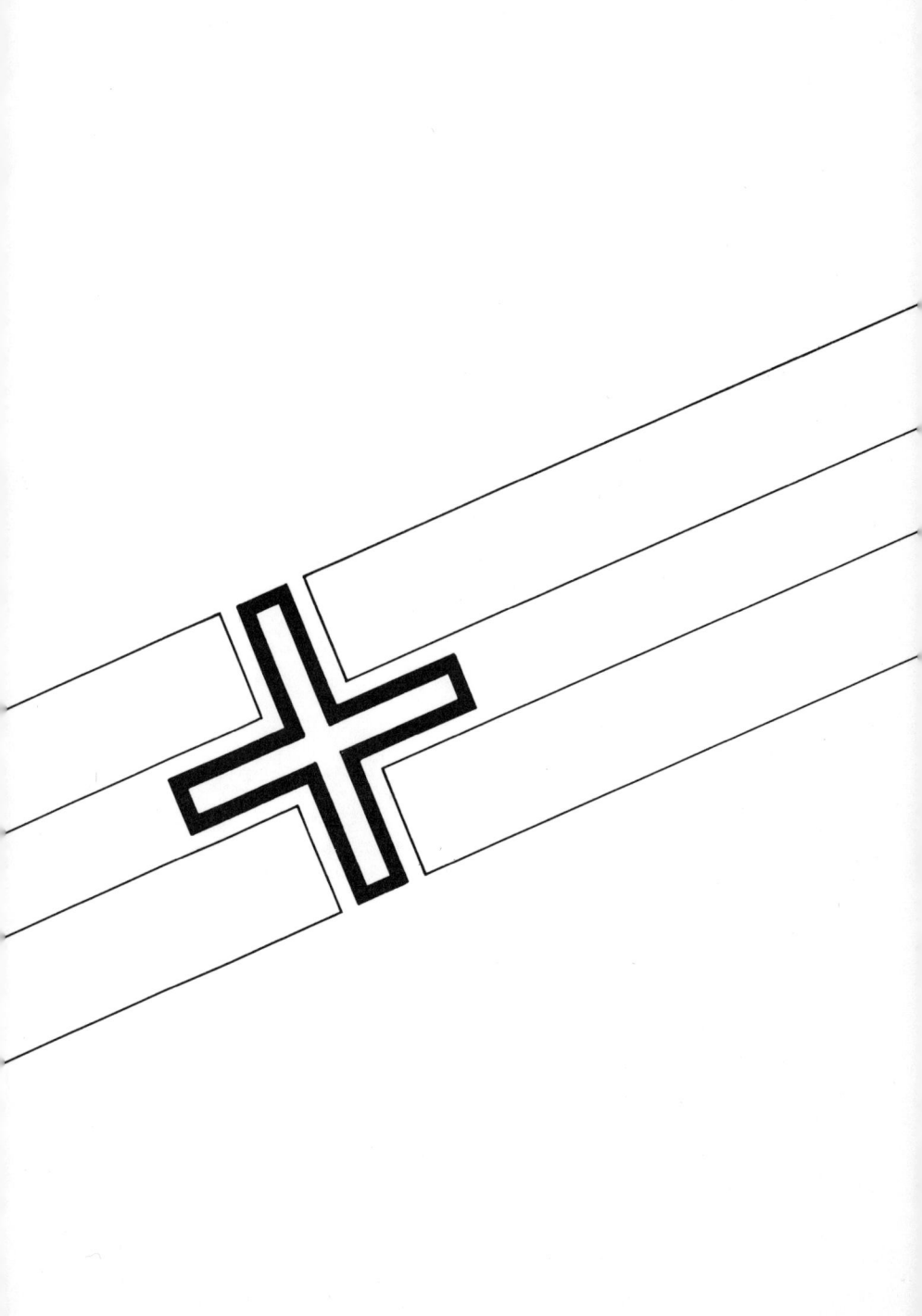

HE NEVER CAME EMPTY-HANDED
St. Andrew, Apostle
November 30
John 1:35-42

Most people can identify easily with Andrew. His name never got in the headlines. He was a quiet worker behind the scenes. Although an apostle, he is mentioned as taking an active part in only three events during Jesus' entire public ministry. Obviously he is a lesser known saint. Yet the Christian world pauses on November 30 each year to remember this man and reflect on his role as a first follower of Christ. Indeed, the billion Christians on earth today are all spiritual descendants of Andrew in their discipleship to the Messiah. Three significant things can be noted about this pioneer believer.

First, Andrew kept bringing people to Jesus. Each of the three times recorded in the New Testament when Andrew swung into action, he is leading someone to Christ. In the gospel appointed for this day, he brought his brother Simon to Jesus. When over 5,000 famished people were growing faint in the wilderness after long teachings by the Lord, it was Andrew who brought to Jesus the boy with five barley loaves and two fish, which Jesus multiplied to feed them all. When some Greeks were in Jerusalem at festival time and wanted to see Jesus, Andrew together with Philip took them to Christ. The most characteristic thing about Andrew is that he kept bringing others to the Lord.

However, this would not have been the case if Christ had not first taken some startling initiatives toward Andrew. One day, right out of the blue, Jesus drew near to Andrew and an unnamed person, both disciples of John the Baptist, while they were standing around with John. The record specifically states that they were standing and Jesus was moving. God made the first move toward Andrew. When John the Baptist announced in the hearing of his two disciples about Jesus, "Behold, the Lamb of God!", Andrew and the other person had the good judgment to start walking after Christ.

Thereupon Jesus took the second initiative. He turned and addressed them, asking, "What do you seek?" At the very start of his public ministry Jesus could have been lost in his own thoughts or too busy to stop and turn around for every hanger-on. Instead he did them a favor by asking a profound question, "What are you looking for in life?" They answered by asking where he resided. Apparently they wanted to come and talk with him some day about such things. Amazingly Jesus proposed doing it that very hour. What a gracious initiative that was! Not only so, but Christ gave them the rest of the day. It was four o'clock in the afternoon when they met. Jesus worked overtime that day, probably far into the evening.

Divine Initiatives at Work

Andrew was so gripped by the person and truth of Christ that the very first thing he did the next morning was to find his brother Simon, announce breathlessly to him, "We have found the Messiah," and bring him to Jesus. Now the Lord displayed another initiative of love. Not only did he give Andrew further time on this second day, but he gazed deeply into Simon's innermost being, saw his vast potential and renamed him Peter, meaning a Rock. Considering that Andrew seemed to be just an ordinary, garden-variety fellow, it is astounding that Christ at the difficult start of his public ministry spent so much time with him. This must have overwhelmed Andrew, too, and commenced the most extraordinary relationship of Andrew's life. Another word for these divine initiatives is grace—God's unmerited goodness. Andrew became what he was because of divine grace.

This in turn prompted Andrew to bring others to the source of his own life's transformation. See how Andrew had grown. When he first addressed Jesus, he called him "Rabbi." This simply meant teacher. When he burst upon his brother Simon the next day, he exulted, "We have found the Messiah." This meant the anointed one, the king. It is impossible to know how much freight the title "Messiah" carried for Andrew at this point, but it was generally understood to mean God's long-promised Deliverer, the greatest person in history. Overnight Andrew had grown to believe in Jesus as the King of grace. He would not let another sun go down before he brought the one he loved most to the same supreme discovery.

Andrew practiced home missions and world missions. He started at home and brought his brother. Some would have overlooked one so near. A believer once asked the famous preacher, Charles Spurgeon, where he should begin in bringing another person to Christ. Spurgeon asked what his work was. "I am a railroad engineer," the man replied. Spurgeon asked, "Is your fireman a Christian?" The man said that he didn't know. "Go and find out," the preacher advised, "and if he is not, begin with him." Begin with your relative, your neighbor, your associate, your friend, your classmate. If you love such a person, help that person to discover also the best in life in Christ. In many congregations the group of evangelism lay visitors is called the St. Andrew Fellowship. Andrew was a fisherman. Christ turned him into a fisher of men. A survey in a Houston suburb revealed that 35% of church members became such because friends and neighbors invited them. No other cause accounted for such a large percentage.

But Andrew was also a world missionary. He brought Greeks to Jesus. In Bethsaida, where Andrew grew up, Jews and Greeks shared the same community. Today the whole human race is a global village which shares the same planet. We belong to one another, and God meant all to belong to Christ. The church exists to proclaim to the world, "We have found the Savior!" The potential response can boggle the mind.

In the interior of Ethiopia in the 1930s a Protestant mission society baptized a few people in the Wolamo tribe and started two of these converts in the neighboring Kembatta tribe as lay evangelists. Then the Italian invasion forced the mission workers to leave. When representatives of the mission society returned to Ethiopia after World War II, they found that those two men, together with a brother of one of them, had won about 50,000 Wolamos and Kembattas to faith in Christ. One tradition claims that Andrew became a missionary to Scythia, another to Achaia. Both could be right. As the first apostle who followed Jesus, Andrew was always bringing others to the Lord. It is the natural response of any Christian who has made the soaring discovery of God's saving grace in Jesus Christ.

Playing Second Fiddle

A second thing about Andrew is that he was content to serve in the background without recognition. He lived in the shadow of his famous brother, Peter. Although he brought Peter to Christ, from then on Peter was the one in the limelight. Andrew didn't mind playing second fiddle in the apostolic orchestra just as long as Jesus was magnified. Andrew must have caught something of this spirit from his first leader, John the Baptist, who said with reference to Christ, "He must increase, but I must decrease."

Andrew was just outside the inner circle of the apostles, consisting of Peter, James and John. He is always listed in the

New Testament among the first four apostles, but never among the first three. Because he was Peter's brother and the apostles are listed in pairs, he made the first four, but he rode on Peter's coattails into the first four. He is even identified on the pages of scripture as "Andrew, Simon Peter's brother." A lesser man would have resented being edged so far into the shadows even unintentionally by his brother. Never Andrew. He was content to labor tirelessly behind the scenes for his Lord while others bowed to the applause.

Behind every great person there is at least one supporting, lesser person hidden by the shadows. Peter had his brother Andrew. Paul had Timothy. Robinson Crusoe had his man Friday. Helen Keller, victor though blind and deaf, had Anne Mansfield Sullivan, who patiently taught her to read and write and speak, accompanying her for nearly fifty years. All cannot be leaders. Some have to be followers. Andrew was content to be a follower. Recognition didn't matter. The only question: Is Christ being magnified?

Andrew had no pretentions to grandeur. While other apostles squabbled shamelessly over recognition, he got on with his loving service to his Savior. When a certain new American ambassador presented his credentials to the French government, he was met by the remark, "Ah, yes, you replace Benjamin Franklin." "No, sir," the ambassador retorted, "I succeed him. Nobody can replace him."

Today Christians in three great nations look up in a special way to the man who toiled in the shadows for his Lord. The Christians of Russia claim Andrew because one tradition holds that he worked in Scythia. The Greek church identifies with Andrew because he brought Greeks to Jesus. The church of Scotland chose Andrew as its patron saint. The shadows could not imprison forever the self-effacing disciple. God honored him by elevating him. The church has designated one of the 365 days a year with the salute "St. Andrew, Apostle."

A Martyr's Crown

Andrew, evangelist for the Lord. Andrew, second fiddle for Jesus. Yes, and now the consummation. According to tradition, Andrew sealed his faith in God with his death as a martyr. This is a third thing about Andrew. He did not shrink from laying down his life for his Redeemer. November 30 has been remembered each year since the fourth century as the day of his death.

A saint's day is not on his or her birthday, but on his or her death day—the day of birth into everlasting life by the mercies of God. The tradition that Andrew was put to death on an X-shaped cross on which he was bound, not nailed, to prolong his dying, dates back only to the fourteenth century. The important thing is not how he died, but that God used the witness of his death to spread the faith.

Every time we meet Andrew on the pages of scripture he is taking a risk for Christ. When he broke into Peter's bedroom early in the morning, dancing with the thrill of a fresh discovery, bubbling, "We have found the Messiah," he could have been thrown out of the room by the big fisherman for such a preposterous claim. When he brought the boy with a little lunch bucket to Jesus while thousands were weakening with hunger in the wilderness, he could have been laughed right out of court as a simpleton. When he brought those Greeks to Christ during the final crowded days of the Lord's short life, he could easily have been rule out of order. But Andrew risked repeatedly for the Lord because the Lord had given all for him. He remembered what Jesus said to those Greeks who apparently wanted to rescue him from an early death and offer him a high position among them as an escape instead. "Truly, truly, I say to you," Jesus answered, "unless a grain of wheat falls into the earth and dies, it remains alone; but if it dies, it bears much fruit. He who loves his life loses it, and he who hates his life in this world will keep it for eternal life."

There are more martyrs for Christ in the present age than in any previous time in history, it has been estimated. It never was safe to be a close follower of Jesus. God deserves risk on the part of believers—the risk of ridicule from worldly persons for being faithful, the risk of lowered resources from giving away generously, the risk of being considered odd by a secular society, the risk of being rejected for witnessing to Christ. But then, the Son of God risked and lost his life for the world because he loved every person in it and would stop at nothing to deliver all.

Andrew has something to say to this age. It is just as true on August 17 or April 9 as on November 30. Keep bringing others to Christ for the most ecstatic discovery of life. Melt into the background in Christian service so that Christ can fill the foreground. And don't shirk from risk because only the seed that dies to itself can live for the Lord.

A travelog book by Laurie Lee bears the title *I Can't Stay Long*. A martyred Andrew concurs in the uncertainty of life's span. Use the fleeting days of this earthly pilgrimage to keep discovering the Messiah ever more rapturously and to bring others to him while working in the background, willing to risk all.

ROBERT W. STACKEL, Director
Love Compels Action/World Hunger Appeal
LCA—New York

FAITH IN GOD IS NOT ENOUGH
St. Thomas, Apostle
December 21
John 14:1-7

Thomas has a doubtful reputation. That is, he is generally believed to have been full of doubt. And there is a degree of truth in this. He should have believed in the Resurrection. Instead, he demanded the evidence of his senses; he wanted to see and touch our Lord's living body. You might say that this disciple, 2000 years ago, had the scientific spirit. He demanded physical demonstration of reality. This then might be a more accurate and more just estimate of his approach. He wasn't hostile to spiritual truth; he wanted to make it concrete. And in this he was much like many of us today, who are literally immersed in the discoveries and inventions of science. We are a people who have put to use all sorts of truths which were hidden from our ancestors. We have demanded to see the previously unknowable, and in thousands of cases we have been successful in our quest.

Ignorance is disturbing, frightening. Until we arrive at certainty we are in a state of anxiety. We are afraid of the future because we don't know what is going to happen and because experience teaches us that whatever it is, it is likely to be bad. Sometimes we become very fearful indeed, when there has been a build-up to a crisis, like a lingering illness which almost certainly will be fatal. Even when our guard is up, we know that the blow will fall and that it will be devastating.

The Troubled Disciples

So the disciples of our Lord must have felt during that last week in Jerusalem. In their hearts and minds was a great foreboding. Jesus had warned them of what was to come quite explicitly: "The Son of man will be betrayed into the hands of wicked men and be killed." What then? What would happen to his followers? Would they be next? What would become of all their hopes and dreams? It was profoundly unsettling. Then Jesus, understanding their anxiety, reminded them to fall back on their traditional faith: "Let not your hearts be troubled. You believe in God. . . . " Some people spell the name of the supreme Being G-O-D; others call him Yahweh, still others Allah. In this connection it does not greatly matter; what does matter is people's trust in divine providence. The Jews, of course, had received revelations of this God which other people had not; they were the chosen people. But for all these revelations God remained invisible, inaudible, intangible. "No one has ever seen God," says St. John, and this was Thomas' trouble, and is ours. We, as sensible people, want the evidence of our senses.

Well, the Christian Gospel says we can have it. Jesus did not stop with saying, "You believe in God." He went on, "Believe also in me." And he was a physical reality. The disciples could see him, hear him, touch him. So, of course, could his enemies. To believe in him was not to look at him, but to accept him as the incarnate God, to recognize that the invisible supreme Being had chosen to come among men as a man and so to accommodate himself to their need of tangible demonstration. He was not just what he appeared to be. There was a hidden reality, revealed only to people of faith. But faith, when it was born, rejoiced to see the enfleshment of that God whom men had always wondered about. The scientific spirit could be satisfied by seeing Jesus Christ.

The Incarnation

There is then this concreteness in Christianity which makes it unique among the religions of the world. It does more than proclaim a God who is purely spiritual, unknowable, remote, but a God who took on himself our nature and dwelt among us, living our life and dying our death. He was born in a place called Bethlehem, at a time when Caesar Augustus sat on the throne of Rome, of a woman whose name was Mary. It is all very specific; it insists that not in any one of an array of wild-eyed prophets, but precisely in this man, Jesus, dwelt all the fullness of the godhead bodily. It narrows down the object of our faith; it says, "You believe in God" (most people do); "believe also in me." So Jesus Christ meets our need for sensate evidence of the existence of God—and of his grace and truth as well.

He also addresses himself to our persistent questions about the meaninglessness of life. What's it all about? Does it have any discernible purpose? Is there any hope for a better world? Jesus says there is: "In my Father's house are many rooms." This of course is picture language. The city of God (itself a metaphor) is not a plush suburb, with one estate more breathtaking than another. What our Lord is trying to convey is that for his people there will be on the other side of death such things as love, joy, peace, fellowship, rest—all those things which we like to think of as being centered in home and family. G. K. Chesterton puts it well:

> To an open house in the evening
> Home shall men come,
> To an older place than Eden
> And a taller town than Rome,
> To the end of the way of the wandering star,
> To the things that cannot be and that are,
> To the place where God was homeless,
> And all men are at home.

The Hope of Glory

Life would be definitely meaningless without the prospect of a consummation like this. Just to plod along from day to day with nothing but death and the grave as the final outcome of it all—this is to be of all men most miserable. But if somehow, mysteriously, God is in control, having conclusively demonstrated this in the resurrection of his Son, then life does have a goal: a new life after death, the kind of life which the disciples beheld in their Lord during Eastertide: "Press toward that goal, then," says Jesus; "let nothing deflect you from it. The great consummation lies ahead; the final victory is sure." "For he must reign till he has put all enemies under his feet. The last enemy to be destroyed is death."

But once more, the peculiar concreteness of Christianity. Heaven, in the teaching of Jesus, is not some vague state in which all the sensory desires of men will perennially be satisfied; the essence of heaven is this: "Where I am you may be also." "In your presence is fulness of joy," said the psalmist, and that is what is meant here. Rich personal association with the Savior—this is the prospect which is the heart of the Christian hope. Whatever fringe benefits there may be, they cannot compare with this central blessing: to be with Jesus.

However, Thomas, the practical man, had trouble visualizing this. He wanted a road map. "How can we know the way?" he asked. We've never been where you're going, and we don't know anyone who has come back from there. If you come back, you'll be the first. But even you haven't been there yet. So what road do we take?" It sounds as though he was asking for very specific directions, like, "Go down County Road 64 seven miles, turn right, drive 15 miles to Interstate 70, go left on that," etc. Translated, this would mean a detailed guide book for life, a whole library of instructions concerning what to do in every conceivable situation. But this Thomas did not get. Nor do we have it in that holy book we call the Bible. God never intended to spell everything out for us. Instead, he relies on us to use our sanctified intelligence to determine the course to be taken. God restricts himself to the kind of reply Jesus gave to Thomas.

The Answer Is the Person

When Thomas asked, "How can we know the way?" our Lord said, "I am the way." This is a very strange statement. Jesus does not say to us, "I'll show you the way"; he says, "I *am* the way." He himself is the path to be followed. The instructions he gives are not to be separated from his person; they are merely the reflections of his unique approach to life, the expressions of his distinctive attitude. To try to obey his teachings without appreciating his genius is to be some sort of legalist. The essential thing is to be controlled by his Spirit. Then everything falls into place, and one does not really need a law book for guidance. St. Augustine came close to it when he said, "Love God and do what you like," because he knew that if you loved God you would do what *he* liked. To say then, "I am the way" is to indicate the distinctively Christian stamp borne by a life that is controlled by the Spirit of Christ. Such a person has what Arthur John Gossip called The Galilean Accent. You may recognize this by the whole manner of a person's life. Corrie ten Boom, author of *The Hiding Place,* is an outstanding example of this—she and her sainted sister. They walked on the way the name of which is Jesus.

Similar things may be said about the other expressions. Our Lord does not say, "I'll teach you the truth," but "I *am* the truth." The truth is personified in him, and knowledge of it is to be attained by being joined to him; it is not acquired by heaping up *x*-number of credit hours in his university. That does not mean it is elusive or slippery or vague. On the contrary, it is centered in the person of Jesus Christ. If you want to know the truth, spend time in his company. Exercise your privilege of worship. "They who worship him must worship him in spirit and in truth."

Our Lord says, "I am the life," not "I will give you life." Whatever Christian life exists in the world is nothing else but a sharing in the ongoing, unconquered life of Jesus Christ. St. Paul's way of putting it is to say that we are members of Christ's body, all of us parts of the same living organism which is the resurrected Lord. Jesus spoke of the same thing when he said, "I am the vine; you are the branches. Abide in me, for apart from me you can do nothing." The life of Christ, then, is to be found, seen, and shared in the church, which is animated by the Giver of life. The church is a very real entity in the world. There life begins in Holy Baptism. There it is sustained in Holy Communion. There it is stimulated, enriched, and developed by the constant use of the Word.

The Vital Choice

It is evident from all this that one's relationship to Jesus Christ is of paramount importance. Indeed, our Lord goes so far as to say, "No one comes to the Father but by me." If he is the way, there is no other way. If he is the truth, all other prophets are unreliable. If he is the life, apart from him there is only ultimate death. This is exceedingly hard and fast, uncompromising —so much so that many people have been alienated by it. And yet, when you stop to think about it, that's how it must be. For anyone to insist on his own way rather than Jesus, is sheer arrogance and rebellion. To accept some other truth is to build one's life on a lie. To live some other kind of life is to cut oneself off from that life which is God's. In short, to refuse Jesus is to choose that from which he came to save us. In all consistency it is to embrace anti-Christ. It definitely is not to come to the Father.

You see how everything hangs together. It all rests on what you think of Jesus. If he is in fact what he claimed to be, then the uniqueness of his person and work lays its uncompromising claim on us. It calls for our exclusive allegiance. It demands complete surrender and obedience. If you think that is too much to ask, consider the absolutely astounding assertion Jesus makes in the concluding verse of today's Gospel. He is talking about God the Father, of whom he says, "Henceforth you know him and have seen him." Think of that! "He who has seen Jesus has seen the Father." Have you seen Jesus? I don't mean his physical body, but the recognition which is of faith, as our Lord later on said to Thomas, "Blessed are they who have not seen and yet have believed." If this has been your experience, then, says this amazing verse, you have seen the Father! Does Jesus' claim still seem too extravagant? He is in truth your Lord, of whom you can say,

> Love so amazing, so divine,
> Demands my soul, my life, my all.

HERBERT F. LINDEMANN
Rio Rancho, New Mexico

REJECTED LOVE
St. Stephen, Deacon and Martyr
December 26
Matthew 23:34-39

From the early centuries of the Christian church three festivals of martyrs have been celebrated immediately following Christmas. December 26th is St. Stephen's Day. December 27th is set aside in honor of St. John, and December 28th is the festival of The Holy Innocents, the children of Bethlehem who were murdered at the hand of Herod as he sought out the Christ child.

December 26th is usually known in the English world by the unimaginative name of Boxing Day, the day that Christmas boxes were traditionally given. The traditional carol "Good King Wenceslas looked out on the Feast of Stephen," remembers this day by its proper name. The goodwill account of the carol took place on the 26th, the Feast of St. Stephen. It is possible that the festival of St. Stephen outdates Christmas in Christian observance. It is even possible that this is the actual day of the first Christian martyrdom.

Stephen was one of the original seven deacons chosen by the apostles to supervise the work of the Christian community in Jerusalem. His faith, his zeal, his enthusiasm soon brought him into conflict with some religious zealots. He was brought to trial, convicted, and stoned to death with the consent of a man by the name of Saul, who later became the great apostle and missionary Paul.

We wonder why the church continued to observe these martyr festivals immediately on the heels of the Christmas celebration. Could it be that for the Christians of the fifth and sixth centuries Christmas was more than the observance of the birth of

Jesus Christ? The birth of Christ was a past event, which indeed it was appropriate to observe, but the real concern of these Christians was their present and future relationship to the One whose birth they celebrated. They were concerned about the commitment of the person who claimed allegiance to Christ. Was he ready to "take up his cross and follow" after his Lord? Was he even ready to go to death for the sake of the faith he confessed? Having come through several centuries of sporadic and sometimes intense persecution, Christians of the fifth and sixth centuries had not forgotten the cost of discipleship.

But there was also their hope for the future. They were looking for their Lord to return, as Christians of every age have done. Just as Jesus had come once, he promised he would come again. In these post-Christmas festivals they were celebrating the communion of saints, the consummation of the kingdom, the glory of the life to come.

The Gospel for today is filled with the pathos of rejection, of spurned love. It sets us back on our heels to make us do some heart searching about what the recent celebration of Christmas has meant to us. Has the flurry of the recent observance brought us closer to the Christ we honor, or have the bright and sometimes flashing lights of the season clouded our vision, so that Christ who came to save has been pushed into the background? Thousands of people in our community have tried again to celebrate the season with no thought of its purpose and significance. They have not worshiped. They have not remembered. They have not honored the birthday of the King!

Today's text is a sobering message for us. It is probably just what we need on the day after Christmas. May the Lord speak to us and strengthen us and encourage us to live out the faith of Christmas each day of the coming year.

God's Patience

First of all today, we would speak about God's patience. Jesus, speaking to the scribes and Pharisees, said: "Therefore I send you prophets and wise men and scribes, some of whom you will kill and crucify, and some you will scourge in your synagogues and persecute from town to town. . . ." He then goes on to mention the blood of two innocent Old Testament victims, Abel and Zechariah. We all know the story of Abel's murder by his brother Cain, the first human murder. The story of the murder of Zechariah is told in the Old Testament lesson for today. In the order of the Jewish Scriptures, 2 Chronicles is the last book of the Bible, and so it is the last recorded murder of one of God's prophets and saints. Jesus refers to the first and last murders as a summary of all the other rejections of his prophets in between.

It's a long tragic story of man's rejection of the God who created him, who sustains him, who provides for his life and salvation. It is difficult to understand why man is so rebellious. Why does he so readily reject the God who created him and loves him? What has God done to incur this rebellion and rejection on the part of his creation? It seems so strange that when someone wants only the very best for us, only the greatest of gifts, only the most blessed of futures that these overtures should be so readily and hastily spurned. And yet, when we look within our own hearts and lives we find the same seeds of rebellion and rejection. There is something within us, inherited from the fall of man into sin, that still seeks its own way, its own will, that does not want to be told what is best and what is safe for the future.

Our own children are a case in point. All good parents anguish over the future of their children. They try to guide them and direct them through the tricky mazes of life in their growing years so that they will have to suffer the minimum of discomfort, but still it seems that each child has to struggle for himself, experiment with the dangerous, play with fire, and sometimes burn his fingers a little while good judgment and experience catch up with him.

The wonder of it all is God's everlasting patience. When one reads the Scriptures one wonders why God didn't give up on mankind long ago. Why does he persevere? Why send prophet after prophet, messenger after messenger, forgiveness after forgiveness? I suppose we will never know, in this world, why God is the kind of God he is. We can only thank him and praise him for the kind of love that went so far that he finally sent his only Son into the world to be our Savior.

The further tragedy is that even though God does forgive man for his waywardness, man still brings judgment upon himself. Our world today bears the scars of man's rebellion against his God. We see it in broken and misshapen lives, in wars and rumors of wars, in poverty and illness, in inhumanity of man to man, and in countless other problems, big and small, that plague our planet. And the question we might ask today is, when history judges us, will its verdict be that we were the hinderers or the helpers of God? That is a question we need to ask ourselves personally, and our nation as a whole.

Jesus' Love

But on this day after Christmas we also need to speak about Jesus' love. The second part of our text today is one of the most heart-rending words that Jesus ever spoke. "O Jerusalem, Jerusalem, killing the prophets and stoning those who are sent you! How often would I have gathered your children together as a hen gathers her brood under wings, and you would not!"

The picture is so simple, so beautiful. In our mechanistic age there are not many today who have seen a hen with her little brood of chicks snuggled under her wings. It's a picture that comes back to me readily from my childhood days on the farm. There is hardly anything more motherly, more comforting, more beautiful in all creation. Imagine a little chick that didn't want that mother's love, that didn't want the warmth and the security of the mother's body and wings.

We all know the pathos of human love that is rejected. We all know what it is to have our pleadings spurned, our love and our concerns set aside by those who are near or dear to us. We can sympathize with the heart of the Savior, bursting with remorse for the rebelliousness of his people. We really know what Jesus is talking about, what he is pleading for, what sadness one human being can bring into the life of another. Our world and our communities this season are filled with similar stories of loneliness, rejection, heart-rending forsakenness. And yet, when all is said and done, who is it that has hurt themselves the most, the rejected or the rejector? It is always the one who does the rejecting. Jesus says, "Behold your house is forsaken and desolate." So it is with our lives. When there is no room for God, no room to love, no room for forgiveness, there is only hollow emptiness.

Our Response

This brings us to our final thought today; our response. I think of the many folks for whom Christmas has been nothing more than a mad scramble for the right gift, filling the house with enough booze for all the parties, trying to celebrate something, they know not what. What is there to take with them in the days that follow Christmas, when the decorations are worn out and pulled down, when the needles have fallen from the Christmas tree, and the place where all the beautiful gifts were is bare, when the novelty of the gifts themselves has worn off, and friends have left for home?

Thank God we can carry more than that with us through the darkness of these winter days. We can carry the brightness of a star that led Wise Men to the Christ child. We can carry this sign of God's eternal love for our world and for each one of us in our hearts and let that radiance fill us and surround us and reflect its light to those about us.

The question of response is ours. We can willfully enter a new year on our own, without God, without grace, without forgiveness, or we can open our lives to Christ's gracious invitation to let him gather us under his wings as a hen gathers her brood. Is there really any alternative? Is there really any logical way to go, than Christ's way?

Stephen, whom we honor today, went Christ's way. He found life in the midst of hatred and cruelty and death, a life opened up for him by his Savior, promised by his Lord, given to him because of his faith.

We do not know what the future holds for any one of us in these last days of an old year, but one thing we know, and that is if we put our hand into the hand of Jesus Christ and let him lead us, there can be only joy ahead. May you know that joy! Amen.

LAWRENCE R. LIKNESS
Zion Evangelical Lutheran Church
Saskatoon, Saskatchewan, Canada

MEET THE FISHERMAN THEOLOGIAN
St. John, Apostle and Evangelist
December 27
John 21:20-25

Quite a Fisherman

This morning I want you to meet the fisherman theologian. We know what fishermen are like and we may be fishermen ourselves. This man was, first of all, a commercial fisherman. He earned his living by fishing. With his father and his brothers he owned a small fishing fleet, had a number of hired hands, and worked the sea of Galilee in the days of Jesus. "Zebedee and Sons of Galilee," together with Andrew and Peter, the brothers from Bethsaida, distributed fish in Capernaum and Bethsaida and possibly even in Jerusalem. They did well enough so that Zebedee and his wife, Salome, had servants in their home and occasionally threw some nice parties there.

So the man I want you to meet and know more personally was a workingman. He worked early and late and braved the sudden storms on Lake Galilee to bring home food not only for himself but also for others. He had the strength, skill and insight fit for a fisherman.

You know fisherman Peter—Peter, the rock, but the man of whom I am speaking is fisherman John, the theologian. Like Peter John followed Christ. Like Peter he was an apostle. Like Peter he is recognized as an evangelist. But more than any other apostle or Gospel contributor John is the fisherman theologian.

More Than a Biographer

A theologian studies God and his relation to people and the world. A theologian reflects on the contents of faith. He seeks deeper understanding, greater clarity and more conviction. With these he helps others both to understand and to believe. He helps the rest of us to see things whole and to apply the Christian faith to daily life.

Fisherman John is such a theologian; in the Gospel according to John he provides us with more than a record of events and more even than a testament of faith. As a close follower of Christ he was open to the deepest meaning of Jesus' life and ministry. That is what he offers us.

Throughout a long life of following Christ, from days of youth to old age, John experienced the Lord's glory and ministered in his name. Then, out of this personal relationship he dictated the material of the book from which today's Gospel lesson is drawn. The fisherman theologian wrote as a believer in Christ to inspire others to have faith in Jesus as the Son of God. He wrote as one who had found life in Christ in order that others also might have life in his name.

> These are written that you may believe that Jesus is the Christ, the Son of God and that believing you may have life in His name (John 20:31).

Follow Me!

John wrote as one who followed Christ in order to inspire others to follow him. The lesson for this festival is that following is the active, expressive element of a believer's relationship with Christ. A person's relationship with Jesus Christ is one of faith, love and *following*.

But following requires discipline. Many things can call for your attention and mine. Our curiosity can get us up tight about many things; but Chapter 21 of John's Gospel reminds us of the main thing—our personal relationship with Christ—and the importance of following him. Concerning many things, the Lord must say to us as he said to Peter: "What is that to you? Follow me." Mind your own business. Mind your real business. Follow me!

Fisherman John deserves our attention because he made a profession out of following Christ. He made it a life-time calling through all kinds of situations. In the midst of this following, the Lord taught John many things and transformed his personality. Along with Peter and James, John was one of the three disciples who formed an inner circle among the apostles. These three were with Jesus during crucial events of his life on earth, for example: when he raised Jairus' daughter, then on the mount of transfiguration when Jesus met with Moses and Elijah, and finally during the agony of the garden of Gethsemane.

At the Last Supper John sat next to Jesus at the table and asked which of the disciples would betray Christ. After Jesus' arrest John followed him into the palace of the high priest. He is the only apostle mentioned as present at the crucifixion. Later, John ran with Peter to see the empty tomb. With Peter he was imprisoned for preaching the resurrection. Later he became overseer for seven churches of Asia Minor. Then he was exiled to the isle of Patmos. But as tradition has it, finally he was allowed to return to Ephesus where he lived the rest of his life. There he dictated the material that became the Gospel according to John.

You see, John was a close follower of the Good Shepherd, of Jesus the Son of God. Through this following he learned many things and truly became a new man.

Memorable Descriptions and Revelations

The fisherman theologian learned from Jesus a deeper meaning in simple things. Jesus spoke in parables. He compared himself and the kingdom of heaven with things of daily life. In these simple things John saw memorable descriptions of Jesus Christ and revelations of his glory. To him Jesus was and is "the Word" —the message of God, God come as a human being to live among us, full of grace and truth. For John Jesus was "the life," the life that is light for people, light by which to live and grow, light by which to relate with others and reach heaven—"the true light that enlightens every man."

For John the Lord was and is "the true vine," of which we are the branches, from which we draw our life and by which we bear fruit. Jesus also is "the bread of life," "the true bread from heaven," which gives life to the world. "He who eats this bread will live forever." Jesus is "the door" by which if we enter we shall be saved. He is "the way, the truth and the life." He is "the good shepherd." No other Gospel writer conveyed so well these simple yet profound recognitions of the nature of Christ. His fellowship with Christ was honored and intimate. As Otto Hophan wrote, "Peter had the keys to the kingdom; John had the keys to secrets of Jesus' heart."

Son of Thunder and Apostle of Love

When John and James first began to follow Jesus, Jesus nicknamed them "Boanerges," which means sons of thunder, sons of tumult. These virile, vigorous men were vehement and impetuous, quick to express strong emotions and desires. They were "sometimes a whirlwind of enthusiasm and sometimes a tornado of wrath." Once when a certain village rejected Jesus, James and John wanted to call down fire from heaven to destroy the town. On another occasion they wanted Jesus to guarantee them places of greater honor and authority in his kingdom than would be given to others.

But later, at the cross, Jesus entrusted his mother to John and John accepted the charge. John had become a man to trust—a man who could love and receive love.

His close following of the Lord taught him not only the importance of following but also the importance of love. He learned this lesson so well that often he is referred to as "the Apostle of Love" and "the disciple whom Jesus loved." No wonder John remembered that Jesus told Peter: "Mind your own business. Follow me!" If we focus on Christ and go his way, we learn love—love for God, love for others and love for ourselves.

Time after time in his writings John spoke of what Jesus had taught him about love.

> God so loved the world that he gave his only Son, that whoever believes in him should not perish but have eternal life (John 3:16).

> For this reason the Father loves me, because I lay down my life, that I may take it again (John 10:17).
>
> If a man loves me, he will keep my word, and my Father will love him, and we will come to him and make our home with him (John 14:23).
>
> He who does not love does not know God; for God is love (1 John 4:8).

These are only a few examples but they make the point.

St. Jerome tells that when John was back in Ephesus as an old man, he sometimes would preach to one of the congregations. News of the event would be widely publicized. After all, John very likely was the only surviving eyewitness who had known Jesus during his physical life on earth. Also John had come through imprisonment, persecution and exile. So on the appointed days many persons came. Always John's message would be the same—about love, God's love for us and our love for one another.

On one occasion John was so feeble he had to be carried into the place of worship. After warm words of welcome and a lengthy opening service, John was lifted to his feet. Silence came over the congregation. Everyone waited to hear. Then in a voice trembling with age but great with conviction, John said, "Little children, love one another. Love one another." That was his entire message!

This John had learned by sticking to the business of following Christ. Thus he became a truly lovable man—able to love and to be loved.

Glory and Grace Now

For many other reasons we are grateful for the fisherman theologian and his message. No other New Testament author saw so vividly the glory of God in the face of Jesus Christ before the resurrection as well as after it. No other saw so clearly that the events of Jesus' earthly life were not only events but also revelations. They were both historical and theological. They were both human and divine. They were events full of power both for showing us the Lord and for inspiring faith. Jesus' ministry lasted perhaps 1,000 days. Of those days John needed only about twenty to point to Jesus' eternal glory and grace.

The fisherman theologian blesses us also with a sense of Jesus' continuing significance. Jesus not only lived once upon a time. Jesus not only will come again. Jesus lives now. His love is a fact of the present, not only of the past and of the future. The true light enlightens. Whoever believes has eternal life and does not come into judgment.

Because of the gift and work of the Holy Spirit we can be convicted, called and enlightened now. Now we are taught and reminded of the things of Christ. Today the Holy Spirit counsels and comforts Christians; today he unites us, sends us and gives us strength for witness and service. In the midst of today's turmoil and triumph we can walk with the risen Lord and know his peace.

The Secret Made Known

The secret is attending to Christ in trust and love. The secret is in faith that follows the Lord. The secret is in faith that recognizes Jesus as the Son of God and follows his lead in each situation. When we are tempted to wander away after interests that really aren't a Christian's business, our Lord says, "What is that to you? Follow me!"

I, for one, am indebted to John, the fisherman theologian, whose close following of the Lord still sheds Christ's love and truth upon our way.

REYNOLD N. JOHNSON
St. Mark's Lutheran Church
Minneapolis, Minnesota

THE TERRIBLE QUESTIONS
The Holy Innocents, Martyrs
December 28
Matthew 2:13-18

How are we to understand this terrible story? Why does it have to be read at all? Can't we bask at least for a few days in the glow of the Christmas candles, relishing the visions of sugar plums and pondering with Mary the shepherds and the angels and their song of "Peace on earth"? We have sung, "Unto us a child is born," but now we are told that his birth means the death of nameless and countless other innocent children. We'd rather not hear that, but the church sets apart this day and rubs our noses in the story, as it has done in its liturgical calendar since the 6th century. Why subject ourselves to this torture?

Our Alternative Answers

We might, of course, read the text another way and make this a day of rejoicing. It is not only the story of the death of the Holy Innocents, it is also the story of the escape of the baby Jesus. As he does with Moses in the bullrushes, God protects his chosen one from the rage and terror of the world's tyrants. We could properly sing "A Mighty Fortress" today and give thanks that Jesus, the promised prophet like Moses (Deut. 18:15), cannot be overcome by the forces of evil.

Or we could take another tack. In the early church many believed that martyrdom for the sake of the Gospel was a certain ticket to heaven. And so it would seem for these innocent children of Bethlehem. Although unwillingly, they died to protect God's own son, and surely God will receive them into his everlasting care. So we need not worry about them. They live in the eternal joy of seeing God face to face, where there is no more pain or suffering. So we could sing "Children of the Heavenly Father" and quietly praise God who cares for those trampled by the boots of tyranny.

But somehow I fear we cannot do either of those things too quickly today. The crying of Rachel rings too strongly in our ears. Perhaps it is because there seem to be so many of those Holy Innocents in recent memory—the small and unimportant ones done to death by the furious raging of the nations— Wounded Knee, Guernica, Auschwitz, Hiroshima, My Lai, and all the unnamed places where in recent years people have been martyred. Or perhaps the song of victory sticks in our throats because even this Christmas has not put an end to our own suffering, just as it did not for me on that Christmas day several years ago when my grandfather died. Why must it be so? Why did God have to choose this way of suffering to bring his son out of Egypt? Couldn't he have acted without pain and death?

Somehow the suffering of the innocent and of ourselves gnaws at us and makes us wonder whether God is God, or if he is God, whether he is good. Can a good God really be in charge of the history we see around us? Isn't it a mockery to say so? Does Christmas have anything to say to the horrors and sufferings we know all too well?

Two alternatives seem to present themselves here, both unfortunately inadequate. On the one hand, we might argue that God has nothing to do with the death of the Holy Innocents or with any other tragic deaths. These simply happen, inexplicably, as part of the ongoing movement of history. God is not to be blamed—evil human beings perhaps, or unhappy accidents, or an impersonal nature. It's just the way things go. The trouble with this sometimes appealing argument is that it is atheistic. If God lives, he must have something to do with what happens. It cannot be otherwise, certainly not if we take the Bible as our guide.

It is precisely the use of the Bible that leads some to the other alternative, that God has every historical event predestined and foreordained from the beginning of time. We might gain that impression from Matthew's Gospel. Everything (including today's tragedy) seems to be done to fulfill what the Lord has spoken and planned. Jeremiah's prophecy of Rachel weeping for her children is seen to reach through 600 years of time and point in terrible precision to the unconsolable mothers of Bethlehem. The whole story is deliberately patterned after the infancy narratives of Moses, showing the plan and continuity in God's direction of history. But, if foreordained by a good God, why the suffering and pain, especially of the innocent? Must we worship a God who murders infants in order to fulfill Old Testament prophecy? Is God himself locked into a system of death because of his unchangeable plans? The thought is grotesque and fortunately God himself argues against it in scripture. Through Hosea he announces (11:9), "I will not execute my fierce anger, I will not again destroy Ephraim; for I am God and not man, the Holy One in your midst, and I will not come to destroy." "I am God and not man!" In other words, God is not bound by any system, not even, according to Hosea, his own law which demands death for the sinner. That is a marvelous word and one which we, who have seen him break through the system of death itself though the gift of his son, need to hear and remember.

So we wrestle with the problem: God, actively involved in history (Matthew and the whole Bible make clear that this is so), yet history reflecting suffering and death which is painful even to God. A slight change in words in our text indicates that Matthew too saw this problem. In announcing the escape of the Holy Family in Egypt, he uses the standard formula of his Gospel: "This was to fulfill what the Lord had spoken by the prophet . . ." But in referring to the death of the children, the formula is altered: "Thus was fulfilled what was spoken by the prophet . . ." God does not do this terrible act *in order to* make prophecy work out and yet it happens, contrary even to his own will. How can this be?

A Word of Law and Gospel

The answer lies in the mystery of the Christmas Gospel: "The Word became flesh and dwelt among us" (John 1:14). God does indeed enter into and determine the course of history. But the entire biblical witness, from creation on, shows that he does this through his Word. God's Word is spoken. In Christ it enters bodily into human events, and that Word contains all the power of God to move and guide the course of nations and of individuals. But it remains a word—a word to be heard and responded to or, alas, rejected. And it is the interaction between that Word of God and our human response which produces both the joys and the tragedies of our existence.

Consider the word of Jonah to the great pagan city of Nineveh: "Yet forty days and Nineveh shall be overthrown!" But forty days later Nineveh stood. Why? Was God's Word ineffective? No, it had great effect. Everyone in Nineveh repented (even the cattle!) and thus God turned from his judgment. It was just because God was one who would turn from his anger and forgive that Jonah was later so upset. He wanted a God of a system, not a God in a person. The spoken and powerful Word of God contains alternative futures, depending upon human response. The same Word comes as both Law and Gospel.

A Word for History and Governments

And so, in our text, the Word of God has entered history in the baby of Bethlehem. And to those who receive him that event means joy and life and peace on earth. But that same event challenges the power of those who want only to rely on their own authority and their own strength and refuse to accept God's gift in humility. It challenges the Herods of the world, who want to maintain their own domination of history rather than leaving it in the hands of God. And when those Herods respond in their furious rage, the innocents suffer.

We know Herod to have been a most wicked king, who out of fear for his throne murdered even several of his own sons. So the death sentence on the babies of Bethlehem is fully in keeping with his pattern of response. But it is too easy to write this story off as the final horrible act of a deranged king of antiquity. Whenever rulers or governments act out of the arrogance of power and out of fear to suppress the supposed threat of those who are poor or lowly or different the innocents suffer and die. We have seen this throughout history up into our own time. And the text calls us to take the lament of Rachel into our own mouths and to cry out on behalf of the suffering. It calls the church to its prophetic task of demanding justice and of reminding those in power of the greater power of God and of his wrath and his compassion.

A Word for You and Me

But this is not only a word for governments, it is a word for ourselves. And as every Word of God, it comes to us also as both Law and Gospel, both to condemn and to save. We too are those with pride and arrogance, who resist surrendering ourselves and our lives to the will of God. And our rebellion too has its consequences of pain for those we injure and of death for ourselves. The Word of God comes to us and calls us to repentance. It calls us to recognize the authority of God, even in the weakness of Jesus, and to turn and receive life through him.

But, at the same time, we are the innocents—those who suffer in the pain of the world, those who are met by injustice and warfare and hatred. The furious raging of those who would resist the love of God catches us all and we see this world through our tears. And to us God speaks his Word of comfort and hope. Just as he took the Holy Babes of Bethlehem unto himself, so also will he take us. Just as he rescued his son from the tyranny of Herod, so he rescues us from sin, death, and the power of the devil. And now, as we make our way through the valley of deep darkness, he walks with us in the person of his son, Jesus Christ. It is not his will that we should suffer in this life, but in his amazing mercy he has chosen to suffer with us and for us. In a sermon on this text in 1528, Martin Luther said, "The tyrants will finally be brought down, but God's word will remain and will persevere unto eternity all those who accept it in true faith and thereby suffer. May our dear Lord God and Father in heaven grant this for us all through his Holy Spirit for the sake of Christ his dear son." (Weimar Edition, vol. 52, p. 604, trans. by FJG.)

So today we might indeed sing "A Mighty Fortress" and rejoice in God's protection of us and his church against tyranny and we might indeed sing, "Children of the Heavenly Father" and give thanks for his eternal deliverance of the innocent children, but in the face of this terrible text and the suffering around us even in this Christmas season, let us also sing, "The Happy Christmas Comes Once More." For it is God's entry into human life through his incarnate Word which results in the entire flow of human history. And as we see through his son, Jesus Christ, in this all-powerful Word, God means well for us.

FREDERICK J. GAISER
Luther Theological Seminary
St. Paul, Minnesota

HE HAS GIVEN YOU HIS NAME
The Name of Jesus
January 1
Luke 2:21

We were greeted on this New Year's morning by 12, crisp new pages hanging on the wall of life, each of them with anywhere from 28 to 31 clean squares to be filled in with dates, appointments, activities, engagements for the year ahead. The calendar of life! "Sunrise, sunset," sang the old man Tevye from the peasant town of Anatevka, "Quickly the years go by. I can't remember growing older. . . ." He milked the cows each morning and he milked the cows each night—one day was little different from the day before—and so the years went by, the children grew and married, his dream of becoming a rich man was never realized. Another chapter in the death march of humanity was written: He was born, he married, he had children, and he died. That's the way it is in the Book of the generations of Adam (Genesis 5).

We cannot predict today the scribbling that will fill in squares between the sunrise and the sunset of the days ahead. We only know that this new year, as every year before and every year to come, is like the cavern, dark and unexplored, that lies before us in which every step must be a step of faith. Politicians, statesmen, economists along with all the rest of us may lay out plans and voice predictions, but in the merciful arrangements of our Lord the future always is at his disposal and must wait for him to do with it as he is pleased.

Now I don't mean to make this first day of the year sentimental, wistful, or nostalgic. Neither do I mean to toss our greetings like a drunken sailor at a party for a meaningless, vague "Happy New Year!" I have a Word for today—a Word that spells assurance, confidence, joy, peace, and power and whatever other good things you can name to make the year a happy year with whatever it might bring. It is a Word that has become the most important Word of faith in English or in any other language—one Word—JESUS, the name of him who came as Word made flesh.

>And at the end of eight days, when he was circumcized,
>he was called JESUS, the name given by the angel before
>he was conceived in the womb.

JESUS—that's the Word. Jesus—He's the Word. God gave him his name. And God has given us his name.

JESUS—that's his handle. And God has put that handle in our hands. It's the handle by which God came down from heaven to get hold of us again. It's the handle by which we can get ahold of God. To know that Word, to speak that holy name is to identify him as the Lord of heaven and earth before whom every knee must bow. To know that Word, to speak that name is to identify ourselves as subjects of his realm. To know that Word, to speak that name, is to be drawn into an intimate and new relationship with him and with his Father and our Father through his name. In Jesus God has put himself within our reach and he has placed his hand on us to claim us as his very own.

The God of Promise

Do you remember how it was with Moses way back in the Book of Exodus when suddenly as he was tending the flocks of Jethro he received his call from God to save the people Israel from their Egyptian bondage? Then Moses said to God, "If I come to Israel and say to them, 'The God of your fathers has sent me to you,' and they ask, 'What is his name?' what will I say to them?" Moses had to have a handle he could get ahold of to identify the God who called him, a name to separate the true God from the gods who cluttered the imagination of the human heart. So through the years of history God has revealed his name, and by his name his people were enabled to take hold of him, address him, call him on the prayer line, and keep company with him. By his name his people could identify him, for his name revealed not only a convenient title, but the very substance of his character, his faithfulness, his holiness, his majesty. His name expressed his very being. His name expressed the character of his relationship with us and our relationship with him.

God answered Moses in the wilderness, "I AM WHO I AM."

Say this to Israel, "I AM has sent me." I AM! Not I WAS, nor I WILL BE, nor I MIGHT BE, but I AM. The always present God, the God who causes everything to be, "I AM has sent you."

And say this to Israel, "The Lord, the God of your fathers, the God of Abraham, the God of Isaac, and the God of Jacob," and in God's name attached to patriarchal names his people read, "The God of Promise!"

So through the ages of the covenant that God had made with Israel, his people called him Yahweh, spelled simply without vowels YHWH, but a name whose content was the faithfulness of God, the God whose promises could never be forgotten and whose faithfulness could never fail. It is no secret in the history of the covenant God made with Israel that frequently his people could not seem to find the handle as they fumbled through their years of faithlessness and failure, disobedience, rebellion. But YHWH always remained YHWH. The God who gave the promise was the God who stood behind the promise.

The Promise Fulfilled

Finally the promise ripened to fulfillment, and in the fullness of the time God sent his Son to Bethlehem. "Call him Jesus," God had said, "for he shall save his people from their sins." "And at the end of eight days, when he was circumcised, he was called JESUS, that name given by the angel before he was conceived."

In Jesus God has given us his Word again, this time in skin and bones. In JESUS God has kept his promise and has given us the promise:

> that the guilt and power of sin which plays so large a role in life cannot destroy us;

> that however fearful we may see the present we have one who came to be our brother and who goes with us down every road of life to lead us to a certain future;

> that in Christ God has a handle on us even as we have a hold on him on his faithful promise.

No devil can lay claim on us when Jesus is at hand. No death can defeat us when the Christ who died and rose again for us and broke the power of death for us and cleansed out every sepulchre is Lord of life for us. By his forgiving mercy he has taken care of everything that rises from the past to haunt us. By his love he promises to be the shepherd of the flock and lead us safely on the craggy precipices of the years ahead. And as one who went through death to life itself, he will lead us through the valley of the shadow when our own time comes.

That name JESUS is important. Need I say that it deserves a better billing than the billing we have given it. All the purposes of God have been revealed in him. All the character of God has been invested in him. All the mercy and forgiveness and redeeming power of the Lord are focused in this Holy Word. By his name the demons are cast out, the guilt of sin erased, the power of evil broken. In his name disease and death are routed. By the power of his name the gates of hell are barred. And in the purity of that name Jesus, lives are changed and hearts are cleansed and Christian character is born. JESUS is his name. JESUS is the Word. He is the Word that he can never let us go or slip from the embrace of everlasting arms.

And if his name is important, your name, too, and mine are important names. we are the ones for whom he came in love. We are the ones he comes to work on now. We are the ones for whom he will come with a welcome to the presence of the God of Abraham, the God of Isaac, and the God of Jacob, and the God of—
What did you say your name was?

He knows your name! He has you and me identified. JESUS is his name, and in his Book of Life is written your name, too.

ALTON F. WEDEL
Mount Olive Lutheran Church
Minneapolis, Minnesota

FAITH'S ROCK FESTIVAL

The Confession of St. Peter

January 18

Matthew 16:13-19

When worship planning teams in several congregations prepared to celebrate this festival of the Confession of St. Peter, they explored ways to involve the children of those parishes. They reflected on Jesus' words to Peter, "I tell you, you are Peter (in Aramaic and Greek, Peter means rock), and on this rock I will build my church." They then decided to send their Sunday school children on a rock hunt. The children decorated the rocks with words like, "Be a rock of Christ's church!", or

"Jesus, you are the Christ, the Son of the living God!" When the congregation gathered for worship on this "rock festival," the children handed their decorated rocks to the arriving worshipers. For the worship hour they had these rocks in hand.

Before we look specifically at our text, we should know this is a special day beginning a special week. January 18, the festival of the Confession of St. Peter, also marks the beginning of a week celebrated in most churches around the world. This week concludes with another festival on January 25, the Conversion of St. Paul. The festivals of these two great leaders of the early Christian church appropriately mark the boundaries of the week which we call the Week of Prayer for Christian Unity. Other Protestant and Roman Catholic Christians today pray for each other, and our scripture is considered in the context of the unity we have as Christians confessing a common faith in Jesus Christ. Now to our text.

The Personal Confession to the Personal Question

The conversation between Jesus and the disciples begins like many of our conversations as we discuss the beliefs of other persons or religious groups. We ask, "What are their beliefs? What do they say about God?" Questions in contemporary public opinion polls almost sound like Jesus' question to the disciples, "Who do people say that the Son of Man is?"

Two thousand years of history have not silenced those questions. There have always been a variety of public opinions about who Jesus is. However, after the public sample has been taken, it is not enough to say, "That's what the public thinks." As always, public opinion is not enough for our Lord. He never allows us to write a term paper merely listing the various points of view. Always at the end, he asks: "Now, what do *you* think? Who do *you* say that I am?" He won't allow us to retreat into uncommitted, objective philosophizing.

Christianity is a very personal thing. Not private, but personal. So the personal question is posed, "Who do *you* say that I am?" Turning to Peter, Jesus shifts from public opinion to personal confession. "Peter, who do *you* say that I am?" Peter confesses with words bigger than he comprehends, "You are the Christ, the Son of the living God."

With Peter, we are called to be a confessing church. Corporately and singly. In our liturgy, the confession of faith follows the word of God coming to us through scripture readings and the sermon. Every time we confess corporately that "I believe in God the Father, God the Son and God the Holy Spirit," remember that you join with Peter and the whole Christian church of all times and places. We are a confessing church.

Celebrating the Rock

When Peter makes this confession, there is reason for celebration! Simon is given a new name so that he is now called Simon Peter or Simon Rock. "I tell you, you are Rock, and on this rock I will build my church."

Throughout the scripture, rocks stand for something strong and secure. They protect or provide a foundation on which to build. God is celebrated as our rock in the psalms. From Psalm 71 there is this prayer, "Be thou to me a rock of refuge, a strong fortress, to save me, for thou art my rock and my fortress."

Jesus builds his church on people who make such confessions of faith. In Ephesians 2, the church is pictured as a spiritual temple made of rocks "built upon the foundation of the apostles and prophets, Christ Jesus himself being the cornerstone."

The church is like a European cathedral, always being built but never completed. Ephesians goes on to speak of us as part of the building program where we "grow into a holy temple in the Lord; in whom you also are built into it for a dwelling place of God in the Spirit." This same Peter, the Rock, writes in his First Letter, "Come to him, to that living stone, rejected by men, but in God's sight chosen and precious; and like living stones be yourselves built into a spiritual house, to be a holy priesthood to offer spiritual sacrifices acceptable to God through Jesus Christ."

What began as especially a festival of Peter, the Rock, ends up being a festival of celebrating all those around the world who are built into the one, holy, catholic and apostolic church of Christ. You and they are the stuff of which God still builds his church. You, too, are named "Rock."

While we celebrate all the varied rocks of Christ in the church, we do celebrate Peter in a special way today.

In the Old Testament, Abraham is seen as the rock from which Israel was hewn and the quarry from which Israel was dug. Isaiah says, "Look to Abraham your father and to Sarah who bore you; for when he was but one I called him, and I blessed him and made him many." As Jesus makes a new beginning with the new Israel, he calls Peter to be the rock on which he will build the new Israel. Peter is for the New Testament people like

Abraham was for the Old Testament people of God. And so, we celebrate Peter, the Rock, one of the foundation stones of the church.

Built on a Rock

As we rejoice in the building of the church from rocks like Peter and ourselves . . . as we think about how Peter wavers later on when he is asked to confess Jesus in an explosive situation . . . as we think about our own unrock-like qualities, hear the rock-like promise of Jesus. He says about his seemingly fragile church, "The powers of death shall not prevail against it."

The reason we have confidence is not that the strength resides in ourselves. Rather the confession of Christ, the Son of the living God, is our strength and security, our rock and fortress.

It is in that common confession, shared by all Christians around the world, which I would invite you to keep at the center of your prayers this next week as we pray for each other in the various Christian churches.

How often we begin with differences between the churches! When we meet someone from another denomination, usually our conversation begins with our differences, "How do you differ from us?" This Week of Prayer for Christian Unity and this text before us can help us pay attention first of all to what we have in common. Think of all the ways in which we are alike. Remember the prayer of Jesus and pray it yourselves that we may all be one as the Father and Jesus are one. We share one baptism, one Lord, one Spirit, one God and Father of us all, one Holy Communion, one scripture, one body and one hope. This is where we should begin and only later, talk about our differences in the light of our unity in God's grace.

And even when we talk about our differences, this rock-like promise should be in our minds, "the powers of death and disunity shall not prevail against it."

At worship when we confess the Apostles' or Nicene creed, keep in mind Peter's confession of faith. These are ancient ecumenical creeds which are shared by most Christians. We have them in common, as we have in common the confession of St. Peter today. There is a oneness in back of our differences. This oneness in Christ we confess even in the midst of this world where because of our sin we don't know how to be one. There is something unseen that binds us together in Christ even though because of our sin, we cannot fully experience that oneness. It must remain one of the main subjects of our prayers.

Built on a rock the church doth stand. Celebrate with Peter

and all the other confessors of faith around the world today as we sing this hymn . . . "we are God's house of living stones, built for his own habitation . . . hither we come to praise his name, faith in our Savior confessing."

MONS TEIG
Director for Parish Worship and Celebration—ALC
Minneapolis, Minnesota

THE DYNAMICS OF CONVERSION
The Conversion of St. Paul
January 25
Acts 9:1-22

The revived concern about death and dying has made it quite fashionable to line up witnesses and testimonials to explain the certainty of some experience of life after death. All of this is nothing new. From antiquity there is voluminous evidence that men have believed in life after death and have recorded experiences with the spirit world and the realm of the dead. Christianity made its debut in Europe at a time when philosophy and culture were very much colored by the conviction that the goal of living and dying was to enter into the spirit world, the world of the gods.

It is an obvious and outstanding feature of the New Testament, however, that it never claimed the philosophical views of the Greco-Roman world as either compatible or friendly to the Christian faith. The New Testament did not need to rely on the popular views of life after death nor the witness of great philosophical minds to bolster or support its witness to the risen Christ. The apostle Paul does not simply proclaim the resurrection of Jesus Christ from the dead, but he makes the resurrection the guarantee of faith. Paul does this because of what he experienced in his own conversion. From this dynamic conversion we learn something about the dynamics of conversion and faith.

Our Synergism

We need not assume that all Christians experience the same kind of stunning confrontation with our Lord as did Paul. The Gospels relate a range of experiences for the other apostles as well as other followers of our Lord. Yet, because the conversion of Paul is so sensational, we can detect within Paul's experience a pattern that outlines for us what God does to us when he makes a claim on us. Paul's bizarre encounter with the power of the Gospel permits us to sift out those features which are common for all who have come under the persuasion of God's Spirit.

To begin, we can recognize in Paul the synergism that is common to humankind. "Synergism" is a word that has dropped out of sermons over the years and is reserved only for theologians. However, it has been popularized in the sciences to describe any two agencies cooperating to produce a greater effect. In theology it means the human effort for man to cooperate with God in working out his salvation. Paul was dedicated to that. He believed that he was doing God a favor when he persecuted those who followed the Lord Jesus. He led the persecution against them. He was willing to carry his cause all the way up to Damascus, 140 miles north of Jerusalem. He demanded from the high priest letters to authorize him to carry on his cruel campaign against both men and women who believed on the Lord Jesus.

God Moves on His Own

Paul's intense synergism, his desire to cooperate with God, represents the same kind of natural effort folks put forth to save themselves. Some people are consumed by the notion that they have to be right. Some think they must be pious. Others think they have to get out of life all they can. Still others think they should sit tight and do nothing. But what is common to all is that they determine for themselves what the course of action should be. Paul's case history reflects for us that self-styled piety and natural work righteousness by which people hope to justify their existence but which God must overcome in order to get at us. In the instance of Paul, God arrests him on the Damascus Road. Perhaps no other passage in Holy Scripture gets more attention than this one in trying to determine what God did to Paul.

From the description one might assume that Paul had a fit of epilepsy. The later references to Paul's poor eyesight lead some interpreters to believe that the incident left Paul with permanent eye damage. That is not the important part, however. Saul has an encounter with God in which he confronts the Word and the message he had so soundly denounced. He hears and sees something no one else can. The one who thought he saw clearly the will of God now is blind. Yet the one who is now blinded sees that the one whom he persecuted is now his Lord. Whatever any of us experience in coming to know the Christ, what is common to us all is that God does turn things inside out for us and turns things around or upside down.

God Chooses Us

We can analyze as best we can what happened to Paul, but we can only give that final rough description which says that God changed his life by what he did for Paul. And this is true for all of us. For some that may be more obvious than others. However, it does not necessarily mean that one changed vocation, address, or friends. The more important thing to note is that God did it. God chose Paul. Paul did not choose God. God came to Paul. God interrupted his plans and intentions. God gave the Word to Paul. God initiated the action to bring Paul under the influence of his love and grace. The Gospel is not that we decide for Christ. The Gospel is that God has already decided for us.

What God did for Paul, Paul would never have dreamed of doing for himself. Once more we can go back and try to analyze what happened. We may say that Paul had a guilty conscience about what he did to Stephen, the first martyr of the church. We may recall the testimony of Stephen on that occasion and say that is what won Paul. Also, it could be that Paul remembered the testimony of others that had followed Jesus and were in "the Way" as the life-style of the Christians was called. All that is speculation. Paul's own version was that he had seen the risen Christ on the Damascus Road. God had come to him through his Son.

God Calls Us Though a Word

Later Paul's autobiographical description of this moment does not dwell on the uniqueness of the event. Rather, Paul sees his experience of God's grace as a sign that God wants all men to be called into his fellowship. Thus the same Christ who came to Paul on the Damascus Road reaches out to others through the Word, through the Sacraments as his means of touching and changing the lives of others. The same Christ who appeared to Paul still comes as the living and risen Christ in his Word and in his Sacraments. We are no less privileged, no less confronted, and no less overwhelmed by this gracious Word by which he comes to us. For Paul this Word was also a command that took hold of his life. He had to ask what he should do. For the moment the answer was brief and not all too clear. He received orders that commanded him to go to a house in Damascus and wait.

Those were orders that commanded obedience with no explanation.

That kind of Word calls for more than obedience. It calls for faith. So it is always for us when we come under the Word. The Word calls for that kind of faith which gives little explanation of where God is leading us. Often we can do nothing but wait. In faith we respond to that Word which led Abraham out of the land of Ur, or led Jesus to the cross or a Paul to a house in Damascus. By the Word through which God chooses us he also calls us to action. Yet much is hidden from us and we can only react in faith that the one who calls us is Lord. By that call to faith we are restored to that original condition of man in which he lived in relationship with God by trust in his Word.

God Brings Us Into Community

For Paul the instructions were to go to a home in Damascus. God was not to live with Paul in a solitary relationship. God lives with his children in a family, the church. Thus God placed Paul into the Christian community through Ananias. We can well imagine how difficult that was for Ananias. He was called upon to minister to this one who was known to be the archenemy of Christians. However, he overcomes his own protestations and prejudices and goes to the place appointed to meet Paul.

What is worth noting is that when Ananias does see Paul, he greets him as "brother." He ministers to Paul, baptizes him, and introduces him to the Christian community. In the Christian community he also gained acceptance and was given the privileges of the congregation. The Christian faith is not a private affair. Christians are built into community. Christian conversion does not call for isolation, but has need for the congregation. It is in the Christian congregation of community that we minister to one another, give encouragement for the faith and the practice of prayer, partake of the common sacraments and serve together. Privacy is not conducive to the upbuilding of the faith, but rather stultifies and hems in the faith that needs community to be expansive and outgoing.

God Changes the Whole Man

It was in the Christian community that it became obvious what God was doing to Paul. His blindness left him. He was filled with the Holy Spirit. He was baptized into the Christian faith. He ate with his newfound friends. The total man was immersed in a new life and a new situation. How thorough this conversion was is revealed by what followed. After Paul was exposed to the tradition and Word which the Christian community witnessed to Jesus of Nazareth, he engaged himself in concentrated study and devotion. In time he emerged as a great missionary. In humility he confessed that he had no right to be called an apostle, but that he had labored more abundantly than all the others. Though he had been the least, he had become the greatest and therefore the chief among them.

In Saul of Tarsus, who became the great apostle Paul, we have a good example of how God converts people yet uses all of the same intuitions, habits, compulsions, emotions, abilities, and skills to serve his purposes. This man who was a dynamo with enormous capacities for persecuting the church, now becomes God's vehicle for extending the church. In that we should be able to see that when God converts us all, he does not alter us in such a way that we lose former capacities or distinguishing features, but he takes us totally and wholly under the persuasion and power of his Spirit so that we are utilized in his scheme of things. We put our energies to work for the sake of his causes instead of our own.

God Passes It On

In the short time that Paul was in Damascus with the disciples he immediately proclaimed Jesus as the Son of God. That formula at that moment in the early history of the Christian community must have been the manner in which Christians confessed the faith concerning the Christ. It was Paul the apostle who later discovered the fullness of the Gospel and its power as he went about proclaiming the Christ. By his missionary experience he learned that the formulas concerning Christ were not understandable to nonbelievers, unbelievers whether they were Jew or Gentile. To the church he later wrote, "I determined not to know anything among us except Jesus Christ and him crucified."

Yet the crucified Christ is the risen Christ. For Paul was to preach that if "Christ is not raised, your faith is vain, you are yet in your sins." Thus all of the new directions God gave to his new life for Paul all came out of the life, death and resurrection of Jesus of Nazareth. That was to be the heart and center not only of his message, but of his own life. It remains the same today. The lasting power of our conversion and faith in the Lord Jesus Christ is our conviction that the crucified and risen Christ continues to be the life and message of the church. It is that dynamic of our conversion that keeps alive the conversion process in the world.

HARRY N. HUXHOLD
Our Redeemer Lutheran Church
Indianapolis, Indiana

TURTLEDOVES, PIGEONS, AND THE PLAN OF GOD

The Presentation of Our Lord
February 2
Luke 2:22-40

Forty days after Jesus' birth the Holy Family set out on their first trip since Mary's ordeal at Christmas. Although the distance from Bethlehem to the temple in Jerusalem was a scant five miles, it was up hills and down valleys, and the family may very well have walked the entire way. The purpose for this initial trip of our Lord is found in Leviticus 12:2-4, where the Law required that every mother of a male child be ritually purified 40 days after giving birth and that a sacrifice be made to God. It was an ordinary thing to do, one which thousands of mothers had done before, but this day turned out to be extraordinary with dramatic events which may have left Mary and Joseph puzzled, if not shaken.

The Law

Turtledoves and pigeons, two of each—that is what the Law required. Mary and Joseph were devout and God-fearing people who performed the necessary sacrifices. "When they had performed everything according to the law of the Lord, they returned". The first incident in Christ's life, his circumcision, was also a ritual fulfillment of legal requirements. What do these incidents mean? They point to the fact that Christ came not to overthrow the Law or to break it, but to fulfill it. He came in order to keep all the commands of God perfectly, including the rituals of the Old Testament. He did not step outside the limits of the Jewish tradition. He was born under the Law, and so he remained, to redeem those who were under the Law. He did not simply disregard or oppose the tradition—he observed it and fulfilled it.

In the same way he conquered man's two other oppressors, sin and death. He did not negate their powers by declaring them void, or by a miraculous and divine intervention. He conquered sin by becoming sin for us. He conquered death by dying. And the Law's powers he nullified by observing it.

Observing the Law was central to Christ's ministry. It was the occasion for his debate with the scribes. It called forth several parables. He worshiped in the synagogues. He observed the Passover. He paid his taxes. And even in death he was hastily buried that the Sabbath might not be violated. It all began this day with turtledoves and pigeons.

But he did not stop there. He went beyond the ritual to the heart, condemning the letter and following the spirit. "The Son of Man is Lord even of the Sabbath day." He reinterpreted the commandments to include all thoughts, motivations, and intentions. He gave the Law meaning and life. But in so doing he made it impossible for anyone to keep. Even as Christ was giving the Law a new meaning, he was keeping it perfectly for us. God's Law continues to condemn us of wrongdoing and provides us a guide for God's will. But when we falter under its demands, think of the pigeons and doves, which are also sacrificial symbols of Christ's sacrifices which frees us from the need to fulfill the Law. It has been kept for us. It can no longer accuse or condemn.

Toward the end of his life, Christ summed up the Law by saying, "You shall love the Lord your God with all your heart, soul, and mind, and your neighbor as yourself." Love is the fulfillment of the Law. "This command I give you, that you love one another." These are no mere ritual demands, no mere external postures, no husks without a kernel. We slip back under the old law when we merely attend church without worshiping, say words without praying, contribute without offering, and play a game of piety. No more sacrifices of doves, but your entire self is the sacrifice acceptable to God.

God's Plan

Turtledoves and pigeons—they form part of God's eternal blueprint. Centuries earlier the young Samuel foreshadowed Jesus' appearance in the temple. He, too, was born of a woman who seemed unlikely to be a mother. He, too, was presented at the temple as a firstborn male. He was also dedicated to be a prophet of God, and his parents offered a sacrifice of purification. It was not fate or the stars or mere chance that these accounts are parallel. Samuel is a forerunner of Christ and points to him as the culmination of God's eternal blueprint.

In the temple Jesus was met by two other patriarchal figures, Simeon and Anna. Both represented the centuries-old tradition of the Jews. They knew that God had promised deliverance for his people. They knew that God had great things in store for those who loved and worshiped him. They recognized in the Old Testament traditions a dynamic which was moving forward to a great revelation of God in the Messiah, but it remained to be seen how this would come about. As Simeon cradled the 6-week-old baby, he knew. History was focused in this little boy.

In this homely and prosaic account of doves and pigeons there lies a profound understanding of world history. It tells us that there is a mind and a direction behind the course of this universe—not only the cosmos itself, the stars, planets, and forces of nature—but also behind the history of this planet and the people on it. More importantly, there is a direction and a goal for each of us as individuals. Just as God directed the events of Israel for centuries, leading up to this moment in the temple, so he has directed your life and welfare so that his will shall be done. Three times we are told that Simeon spoke as he was prompted by the Holy Spirit. It was not mere chance that directed him to recognize the Messiah and sing his song of gratitude. It was the direction of God himself.

We have heard this comforting message often, yet our own experience prompts us toward skepticism. Our experience may suggest that we are like corks bobbing on the waves of an endless sea. Or worse, that there is a mind behind the universe, but it is capricious, evil, and seeks for our destruction. God's people have often been troubled by these doubts, including Christ's own disciples. But we have also experienced the hand of God through troubled times. To say that God directs our lives is not to say we shall be immune from the slings and arrows of outrageous fortune. Simeon predicted of Mary that even "a sword will pierce through your soul." This, too, was at God's direction. And the sacrificial pigeons and doves pointed to another sacrifice of this little baby, which seemed grotesque at the time, but served God's saving purposes. Joseph, the patriarch, said, "You thought evil against me, but God meant it unto good." Today's Lesson reflects the solid word of comfort which God gave to Jeremiah, "Before I formed you in the womb, I knew you, and before you were born I consecrated you." The original Apostles' Creed refers to God the Father as the "all-ruler," the one who is finally in charge.

The Human Jesus

Turtledoves and pigeons—flapping around a dirty cage and finally thrown on a waste heap. What has this to do with grand designs of an eternal nature? And what has a helpless baby boy to do with the universe? Both are reminders that God works through humble means. His salvation was brought about through a fellow human being, the Son of Mary, whose humility included being carried to a temple where a simple sacrifice was offered. The lesson ends with the notation that Jesus grew and became strong. He ran and played. He did chores around the house. He went to school. Had he been physically among us today, he would no doubt have had a bicycle, peddled a paper route, gone camping, and learned to play a trumpet. God still works miracles, but the miracles are through very ordinary and commonplace people and events.

Sometimes the humanity of Christ is offensive to us. Recently when a new painting of Christ was revealed entitled, "Christ in a Crew Cut," showing him in bib overalls, people were shocked. Members of a Bible class suggested it would be inappropriate to suggest that Christ may have suffered from diaper rash and constipation. This is an index to our overemphasis on his divinity and other-worldly nature. We are so accustomed to having him portrayed with a beatific countenance, surrounded by a halo, gazing into the eternal distance, that we are surprised to discover he was really like us. Today's Epistle reminds us that, "he himself likewise partook of the same nature, that through death he might destroy him who has the power of death . . . Therefore he had to be made like his brethren in every respect. Because he himself has suffered and been tempted, he is able to help those who are tempted." The early church declared those to be heretics who denied the real humanity of Christ, for unless he were truly like us, our salvation would not yet be accomplished.

Furthermore, unless Christ is truly human, we would receive nothing in Holy Communion. Unless he possessed flesh and blood, it is meaningless to say we eat his flesh and drink his blood in the Holy Supper. Today's Gospel is a dramatic reminder that our Lord was indeed like us in every respect.

Salvation

"Mine eyes have seen thy salvation which thou hast prepared before the face of all people." Turtledoves and pigeons point to the coming sacrifice. There is something ominous and foreboding about this event. Simeon predicts that Mary would experience sorrow. Salvation would come, but at a price.

Simeon, the layman, and Anna, the laywoman, were the first to recognize in Jesus the Messiah, though they were surrounded by temple clergymen who remained ignorant about his significance. And Simeon's prophecy included salvation for all, "a light for revelation to the Gentiles and for glory to thy people Israel." It had been prepared "in the presence of all peoples." Even though Christ was the fulfillment of Jewish hopes, foreshadowed by Samuel, and announced in the Jewish temple by a Jewish prophet and prophetess, he was to be the Savior of all people of every time and place. Furthermore, when Simeon declared that he had seen God's salvation, he was referring to a person, to the Christ child. Salvation finally is not in a plan, or a program, or a system of ethics, or a set of rules, or gimmicks. It is found only in the person of Jesus Christ, whom Simeon was holding in his arms. Although this saving person extends his promises to all, some would reject it. He was "set for the fall and rising of many." He forced himself on no one. He would be "spoken against." But to all who receive him yet today, he brings salvation from present maladies and the sure hope of an eternal future with him and all who trust in his word.

Therefore with Simeon we can say, "Let your servant depart in peace." Christ's ultimate blessing to us is peace. "Peace I leave with you. My peace I give unto you. Let not your hearts be troubled. Neither let them be afraid." God has designed amazing things for us out of commonplace events and things. A young mother and her husband, carrying a little baby, came to the temple. There they met two senior citizens who were the first to recognize the Messiah. They sacrificed two turtledoves and two pigeons. Thanks be to God! Amen.

CARL A. VOLZ
Luther Theological Seminary
St. Paul, Minnesota

AN ALMOST ANONYMOUS APOSTLE

St. Matthias, Apostle
February 24
Acts 1:15-26

Half a century ago, an adventurous youth was brutally attacked by the brakeman on a freight train. He realized that the brakeman was attempting to kill him and, despite a sudden revelation that he was stronger than the brakeman—and a consuming rage to retaliate—the young man jumped off the train at the first opportunity. He made his way to a hobo jungle where a tough-looking man asked, "Who slugged you, kid?" They talked a bit until the man went to sleep.

Someone whispered in the youth's ear, "Careful, fella . . . that guy's got a gun. He's dangerous." But the two traveled together, shared food, and the older hobo gave the younger man advice that served him well.

In his autobiographical work with the subtitle *The Excavation of a Life* (title: *All the Strange Hours*), Loren Eiseley relates that he never saw the man again; he never learned his name. But he never forgot him, although he guessed that the man either died in a Chicago flophouse or in a violent gun battle. Eiseley writes, "Years later when the bodies of men like him lay on dissecting tables before me, I steeled myself to look at their faces. I never found him. I am glad that I never did, but if I had I would have claimed him for burial. I owed him that much for some intangible reason. He did not kill the illusions of youth. . . . But he left all my life henceforth free of mobs and movements. . . . I owed him that.

> Before nothing
> behind nothing
> worship it the zero.

Matthias—Almost an Anonymous Apostle

Saints days serve to jog the memory of the church. They remind God's people of the dedicated witness and service of specific persons who have responded in the past to the call of Christ to proclaim the gospel and bless his name. Some saints stir up more vivid memories than others; Matthias means practically nothing to many church members, simply because little is known about him, his life, and his ministry. His name occurs but this one time in Scripture, then he disappears from the holy record of the early church. Matthias had been with Jesus from the beginning of his ministry until his ascension. He had been passed over by Christ when the Twelve were selected by the Lord. The faithful chose him to replace Judas, after his defection and death, as the twelfth Apostle. The Bible says nothing more about Matthias after this, "and he was enrolled with the eleven apostles."

Tradition has it that Matthias was sent to Ethiopia as a witness to the resurrection of Jesus Christ. And tradition also insists that Matthias witnessed as a martyr who gave his life as testimony to the truth of the gospel. On her journey to Jerusalem in the fourth century, the Empress Helena located the body of a man reputed to be Matthias and had it removed to Rome. The bones of Matthias were buried beneath the main altar of St. Mary Major Church, one of the seven pilgrimage churches in the Eternal City where pilgrims may gain indulgences today. That's about all that is known about Matthias; he has no history, no further marks of identity. The body in the confession of St. Mary Major Church is headless (Matthias' head is buried in Trier)! What more is there to remember?

> Before nothing
> behind nothing
> *remember him* the zero.

Matthias' Day Is the Festival of Apostolic Succession

Any excavation of the life of Matthias beyond text and tradition would simply be unprofitable speculation bordering, perhaps, on idolatry and superstition. But Luke makes the appointment of Matthias as the twelfth apostle into the establishment of a democratic process for electing people to Christian ministry. The text reveals the nature of apostolic succession in addition to recounting how the election took place and its result. Apostolic succession is not so much an unbroken chain in ordination by "the laying on of hands" from the age of the Apostles to the present as it is a call by the church to selected and faithful members of the Body of Christ to join the ranks of apostles, saints, and martyrs by witnessing to the resurrection of Christ. It is not merely the assumption of clerical office, rather it is participation in an evangelical function fundamental to the proclamation of the gospel and the coming of the kingdom of God.

The role of those who are called at witnesses by Christ and the church is indivisibly connected to the gospel story. Those who have heard it and believe it are called to tell that story wherever they go in the world. In her book about the Polish priest Father Maximilian Kolbe, who was martyred in World War II in Auschwitz, *The Death Camp Made Him Real*, Maria Winowska tells how she met a man in Paris whom she calls Pierre. Pierre, like Maria, had been in a concentration camp and he was broken in body and bitter in spirit from his experience. Pierre had lost faith in humanity, although he clung stubbornly to an imperfect faith in God. He said to her, "Human fellowship is hell." She asked him, "Do you believe in God?"

Pierre made the following reply: "Yes, I believe that God exists in an inaccessible heaven of heavens, while we poor humans are crawling around in the mud. Grace? Yes, that exists, perhaps, but of what importance is it if it does not succeed in changing man? There are certain miseries where grace has no access."

To Maria's probing, "What of the saints?", Pierre laughed and said, "Why, yes, I believe in the saints . . . but they are products of greenhouses. They need a special climate . . . with sanctifying conditions. Saints do not grow in inhuman soil. I defy you to show me a saint in a concentration camp. One saint. One who truly prefers his neighbor to himself. I defy you." And Maria responded, "Suppose I accept the challenge. . . . If I show you a saint in a concentration camp; someone who offered to die in place of a fellow prisoner . . . what then?"

Pierre listened while Maria told the now-familiar story of Father Kolbe's sacrificial act of taking the place of a condemned prisoner in the infamous Hunger Bunker of Auschwitz. He was so moved by her account of the modern martyr's death that he joined the ranks of those people making petition to the Roman Catholic church for the canonization of Maximilian Kolbe. He became a witness to the life and death of Father Kolbe, relating the story to anyone who would listen to him.

With the election of Matthias to the Twelve, a succession of witnesses to Christ's death and resurrection was begun that has swollen into a mighty army of martyrs and saints spanning the twenty centuries of the Christian era. It is an anonymous, faceless army, for the most part, but the continued existence of the church around the world speaks eloquently of the power and might of its witness.

Renewed Lives Witness to the Resurrection

The most effective form of witnessing to Christ's resurrection has always been in the lives of people wherein the power of his resurrection is demonstrated to the world. The risen Lord has removed the fear of sin and death from his people, but he also renews their lives and makes new creatures out of them right now. The best evidence, some would argue, for the resurrection of Christ is in the lives of those who insist that he is the living Lord. Cardinal Suhard once wrote: "To be a witness does not consist in engaging in propaganda, nor even in stirring people up, but in being a living mystery. It means to live in such a way that one's life would make no sense, if God did not exist." That's why saints and martyrs make the most powerful witnesses to the Lord's resurrection.

If that statement is true, there seems to be little room for contemporary people to move into the ranks of the apostles, martyrs, and saints. Yet all of us are called to be witnesses—and there are various forms of martyrdom and sainthood; one may witness effectively in living, not only by dying, for the Lord. And this means that all of the witnesses must share in a commonness of commitment that counts more to God than cleverness; in a totality of response to Christ's call that means more to the kingdom than human ingenuity; and in a Christian life-style that has more impact upon others than anything else one does or says. Those who live the new life speak the language of faith and love and hope, and there is no more powerful language to be heard on earth. Their lives shape and sound forth their eloquent witness to Christ's resurrection, reign in glory, and his return at the end of the age.

A certain professor was invited to preach in a small, remote parish where a former student served as pastor. The pastor's wife invited the professor and his wife over to their home after the service. "Our youngest son will be down in a moment," she informed her guests. Almost immediately a 3-year-old hurried into the living room. He was dressed in T-shirt and shorts which revealed not only his artificial legs, but the fact that he had no arms, either. Later, the professor and his wife learned that the pastor and his wife had heard about this handicapped child, unwanted by anyone because he had been born without arms and legs. They sought him out, made arrangements to take him home, adopted him and made him their own despite the fact that they knew their life together would be difficult. As they were driving home, the professor and his wife talked about the remarkable sermon they had seen in that rural pastor's family; the risen Lord lived in them and their home continually and powerfully. And the professor said, "I wish I could preach as powerfully as that."

None of us can possibly be named in Scripture with Matthias and the apostles. Few of us will find places in the history books. We are called to take our part in the mission of the church with Matthias—nearly anonymous, almost faceless from a human perspective. And this we believe: there are no faceless ones, no zeros with God, particularly among those who witness in word and deed with the apostles to the resurrection of Jesus Christ. That witness heard around the world, reaches the ears of God.

And God remembers all the witnesses—from Matthias and the Twelve even to you and me.

GEORGE M. BASS
Northwestern Lutheran Theological Seminary
St. Paul, Minnesota

THE GOD WHO WOULD BE MAN
The Annunciation of Our Lord
March 25
Luke 1:26-38

Some time ago I read an unforgettable review of a book I have never seen. The book was written by a professor of religion at one of our great universities. He called it, "Biography of the Gods." Of it the reviewer said, "You will hardly ever find anything so learnedly foolish. It begins with a chapter on the birth of the gods. For all of them alike were born; all alike, they had their origin in folklore and superstition. Emotion, not intellect, mothered them. And all alike, from century to century, they changed, they grew bigger and got better. They adjusted themselves to philosophy, to the moral and social climate. And one by one they died. Until today Allah and Jehovah and Jesus of Nazareth all face the twilight together, with love and justice and peace nowhere in the universe—save in man himself."

I take it that you people gathered here for worship today find that statement distasteful and probably even irresponsible for a professor of religion. Possibly it will serve to point up the fact that there may be a vast difference between the tenets of a given person's religion and the claims of historic Christianity. The fact of the matter is that most of us are inclined at times to style our God according to our own preconceived pattern. We give him our moods, our attributes, our abilities and our likes and dislikes. We make him a Democrat in one part of the country and a Republican in another. Or possibly the two differing convictions are separated only by a center aisle in a given church. He is one who frowns on a certain mode of behavior in 1910 and condones the same in 1977. Little wonder that those outside the church have difficulty in appreciating our claims.

Announcing—God's Invasion of History

There was a tale told once of "the man who would be God." We're all that person . . . striving to stand on the shores of eternity grasping for heaven and dictating what it should be like. But, in the words of Harold Cooke Phillips, "Whenever man tries to be God he winds up acting like the devil." In contrast, the story of Christianity is the story of "the God who would be man." The God who was so concerned about your welfare and mine that he took upon himself the form of a servant. The God who so much desires our salvation that he bears the burden of the guilt for our sins and suffers and dies. The God who is so distressed with the sinful human situation that he leaves eternity and invades human history for the sake of saving it. The God who so dislikes the discord we humans have made out of his harmonious creation that he enters our history by way of putting it back together again. This must have been what Paul meant when he said, "God was in Christ reconciling the world unto himself." The celebration in the church year which we observe today tells how he got there. The Annunciation of Our Lord is the festival which is intended to announce God's invasion of human history and by way of being biologically accurate it falls precisely nine months (March 25) before the festival of our Lord's nativity.

Thus we're dealing here with what is probably the most mysterious of all the miracles of Scripture and the one over which there has arisen more controversy than any other. Was it included by the evangelist Luke by way of repudiating heretical tendencies that were already evident in the early church? There were those who taught that Christ only gave the appearance of being human and that he was really a divine entity, not subject to the trials, tribulations and temptations of ordinary human beings. His biological identity with his mother, Mary, even in a prenatal state would certainly set such an argument to rest. At the same time, there were those who had difficulty believing that there was more here than meets the eye. "Is this not Joseph's son?"

As we learned in a recent Epiphany gospel, it was these same faithful people who had seen Jesus growing up in their midst who had difficulty accepting his identification of himself with the prophet's reference to the coming Messiah. In fact, so enraged were they that they "led him to the brow of the hill on which their city was built, that they might throw him down headlong" (Luke 4:30). Claims about the divine have always given rise to high human emotions and I suppose they always will. This, after all, is at the heart of the Christian message. The people of Israel had for centuries been awaiting God's invasion of the human scene and now one of their prophets, John, was stirring in the womb of his mother, Elizabeth, waiting to herald the coming of the Christ, God's anointed.

True Man and True God

It may be helpful to observe that the most profound issue at this point was not how conception did or did not take place (that issue has been debated among theologians for centuries), but rather, it had to do with the fact of God's active presence through the operation of his Holy Spirit in the midst of life. Could it be that at this early date in the history of the church, a period which precedes the advent of the great creeds of Christendom, the story of the conception and birth of Jesus is Luke's way of establishing the church's faith from the beginning that God had, indeed, come into human life for our salvation in the person of Jesus of Nazareth? The doctrine of the virgin birth which the church has professed through its creeds ever since is for the purpose of saying loudly and clearly that Christ was true man and true God.

The big question to which Luke addressed himself was, "How was God to come?" It is stated very clearly when, speaking to Mary, the angel said, "The Holy Spirit will come upon you, and the power of the Most High will overshadow you; therefore the child to be born will be called holy, the Son of God." Thus the church has confessed its faith ever since in the words, "I believe in Jesus Christ who was conceived by the Holy Spirit, born of the Virgin Mary." How could such a thing have taken place? I don't know. No human knows. But let us not limit God in his activities by the finiteness of our own minds. May we recall, as well, the element of mystery and miracle that surrounds human reproduction.

Human Genes and Divine Genesis

In treating this event in his book *Miracles*, C. S. Lewis has a very interesting and, I think, helpful point of view. He reminds us that human procreation always carries with it the weaknesses and corruptions of the past (a fact of which we are becoming increasingly aware in a day of genetic counseling). In each of us there is something that was also in our forebears and there are even some things unseen that will reappear in our great grandchildren. No human parent begets a completely new individual, because influences out of the past are born out in the new creature. The Scriptures speak with scientific accuracy when they say that the sins of a generation are visited upon many generations yet to come.

Thus, Lewis suggests, we see the reason for Luke's reference to a principle of divine conception in the life that was coming into being in and through Mary, the mother of Jesus. Here was life completely new, like the first Adam before the fall. Able to sin? Yes, because he was also man born of Mary; but, unlike all others born before or since, he was able also not to sin. Here is the impenetrable mystery—that one like us should be able to live in complete obedience to the will of God. Yet his life and ministry bear testimony to the fact that he faced all the trials and temptations we face. His was not an insulated existence that knew no freedom. Thus the Christ event has become the center of all human history, sacred and divine. In the first Adam we all sinned, but in Christ came life and victory over sin and death.

The writer to the Hebrews could therefore say of him, "He is the author and finisher or the pioneer and perfecter of our faith." He did what we could not do, but he shares it with us in and through faith and we become his benefactors in the life of the new community which is his church. This function which befell Christ as Son of God pours its resulting blessings upon us as brothers and sisters of the Christ by virtue of his sharing our humanity. Thus, one can speak of him as the bridge which reunites us with our creator in terms of his original purpose for our lives which we have defiled in our self-centeredness. He it is who restores the fullness of our humanity.

A New Creation

George B. Caird, the famous Oxford biblical scholar and member of the translators panel for the New English Bible, speaks of Jesus taking this father-son imagery and remodeling it in the crucible of his own experience. He uses the terminology not for doctrinal purposes to tell the church what it must believe, but rather to express his own personal relationship to God whom he knew intimately as only a son can know a father. Writing on the specific passage before us today, Dr. Caird says,

> What Luke is here concerned to tell us is that Jesus entered upon this status of sonship at his birth by a new creative act of that same Holy Spirit which at the beginning had brooded over the waters of chaos. It is this new creation which is the real miracle of Jesus' birth and the real theme of Gabriel's annunciation and Mary's wondering awe.
>
> (Pelican New Testament Commentary on *St. Luke*, p. 53)

What all of this seems to be saying to the Christian is that we have not created God in our own image. If he were of our creation, chances are he would not have been a suffering servant. Human dreams about the divine are not apt to be cruciform, but God's revelation of himself to us in Christ is. The Gospel is offensive to natural religion precisely because it begins with an acknowledgment of human inadequacy. In spite of this fact, however, the announcement of this day reminds us that our inadequacy is subject to transformation. God takes bent creation and straightens it out. He uses us, if we will let him, to effect his miraculous change and recreate harmony in a discordant world.

In Him God Is Doing a New Thing

Long years before the advent of Christ, the prophet Isaiah had said that the former things were passing away and new things were coming into being. The people of Israel had lived with this hope for centuries and now in the person of a humble young woman named Mary it was happening. Our focus today has been mainly upon what God was doing in and through this event in history and rightfully so. But we would be remiss if we failed to give some attention to another principal in this action. The young woman whose life became a vehicle for God's advent in human history was more than a passive instrument. God never violates the integrity of the individual. He created us free and that freedom is a large part of his image in us. He uses us only as we give him opportunity. We are not puppets on a string, not automatons, but people . . . people capable of responding to the invitation of the almighty.

And to the message of the angel, Mary responded, "Behold, I am the handmaid of the Lord; let it be to me according to your word." There is nothing in that statement which suggests that she understood his choice of her to have been a result of some special quality in her life that made her worthy for this honor. She is simply addressed as the "favored one, the recipient of a privilege, the beneficiary of God's sovereign and unconditioned choice," as Caird puts it. It is ever the same. God is constantly inviting us to become the agents of his presence in the midst of life, agents who are empowered by him to effect changes that are beyond the expectations of mere humans, for the Holy Spirit is still an operative reality on the human scene.

The God who would be man became one of us and so transformed life before our very eyes in order that we and all humankind might be a part of the new creation. The announcement is still valid: "The power of the Most High will overshadow you, he will reign forever and of his kingdom there will be no end." Can we say, with Mary, "Let it be to us according to his word?"

CLIFFORD J. SWANSON
St. Olaf College
Northfield, Minnesota

SECOND-STRING SAINTS
St. Mark, Evangelist
April 25
Mark 1:1-15

Little Joe wanted to play baseball in the worst way. Unfortunately, he often did. Lacking the skills of a gifted athlete, he held small hope for making the school team. But he tried. When the list of players surviving the cut was posted in the gym, he couldn't believe his eyes. His name was there. The joy was still glowing from his face that evening when he burst through the door announcing, "Dad! I made it! I made the team!"

As days went by, however, the glow began to fade. Scrimmage games showed that Joe would not be a starter. When the season opened, he was warming the bench. A second-stringer! The very name made him feel like a failure.

The Status of Seconds

Do we see ourselves in that story as we strive for stardom in this game of life? We life in a society that values winners. In former days we were taught, "It's not important if you win or lose, but how you play the game." But since then the goal line has changed. Vince Lombardi, former coach of the Green Bay Packers, voiced the value dominant today: "Winning is not everything. It's the *only* thing." Victory has replaced integrity as the yardstick of personal worth. All areas of endeavor are arenas of war and "there is no substitute for victory."

What this means, of course, is that most of us are labeled as losers. There can never be more than one winner in any contest. The very word WIN has the Roman numeral ONE at its center. The division between winners and losers is not found half way between first and last. It falls abruptly between first and second. For the word *second* now means *inferior*. Seconds in merchandise are flawed products not worth the list price. Second-class spaces are cheap places where only cheap people stay. A second-chance is for those who first failed. No wonder feelings of inferiority and inadequacy are epidemic among us.

Just think of all the second fiddles in the orchestra of life. Women have been traditionally recognized only for their role "behind" some great man. Minorities may have worked their way up from the bottom, but are still not acceptable at the top. Faceless millions are thrown crumbs of gratitude under nameless labels like "the little people behind the scenes." These are not only workers with menial jobs. They are also the vice-presidents, assistant coaches, junior executives, under-secretaries, middle-managers and associate pastors. In short, they are the workers who make everything work, without whom nothing would be achieved by anyone. Yet in spite of this, they are treated as though they have not made it and never will make it in life. Nearly all of us are among them.

Is our status in church any different? Today is festival of St. Mark, Evangelist on the Christian calendar. We think of saints as superstars in the religion game. So here we sit, warming the church bench, waiting for Mark to demonstrate how winners perform on Christ's team. But we're in for a surprise. For Mark is the patron saint of second-stringers.

Every scrap of information the New Testament gives us shows Mark in the shadow of some greater player. We meet him first as the son of a wealthy woman named Mary, whose home was the meeting place for Christians. Mark must have been known as "Mary's boy." Then we find him in the shadow of his cousin, Barnabas, the man who brought Paul out of obscurity and led him on the first missionary journey. Mark went along as a helper, but then quit the team after Paul emerged as its leader. When the next trip was planned, Barnabas wanted to give Mark a second chance. But Paul adamantly refused! When Barnabas insisted, Paul broke up their partnership. He would rather go without Barnabas than to go with Mark.

Later we find Mark back on Paul's team, but not as an equal. Paul calls him "my fellow worker" in Philippians, but when he asks Timothy to send Mark to him, it is because "he is useful to me," a kind of second-mate. Finally, we see him in the shadow of Peter who refers to him as "Mark, my son," a warm but junior designation.

It's symbolically significant that Mark's gospel holds second place in the New Testament. Since nearly all of its contents are also found, often word for word, in Matthew or Luke, scholars have assumed for centuries that Mark copied from those more primary sources. Even his writing was secondary stuff.

So, here is a second-string saint if we ever saw one. He was good enough to make the team, but not worthy of much recognition. This is the status of seconds. They are the servants who work in the background, while those in the foreground gather the credit. Mark was one of these and so are most of us.

The Savior of Seconds

Yet, second-stringers have some things going for them. Since they have more work than time to do it, servants waste no effort on nonessentials. That's the way Mark tells the story of Jesus. The fifteen verses that open his gospel cover ground that Matthew and Luke spread over four chapters. The ministry and death of John the Baptist, the baptism and the temptation of Jesus are all reported in rapid order. Then the preaching of Jesus is summarized in a single compact sentence: "The time is fulfilled, and the kingdom of God is at hand; repent and believe in the gospel."

The first half of that sentence tells the content of Jesus' message. "The kingdom of God is at hand." The reign and rule of God is about to break into this world. The only one who ever was No. 1 is taking the controls. Pretenders to the throne have gone as far in running things as the divine patience will allow. The King is at the gate to claim his position of primacy on this planet and exercise his power in it.

Mark calls this message "good news." But it certainly wasn't good news to those holding top spots in the world's eyes, or their own. It wasn't good news to kings like Herod; or governors like Pilate; or high priests like Caiaphas; or religiously elite groups like the Scribes and Pharisees. To this day, it isn't good news to those who think they are capable of controlling their own life and destiny. Winners find this news a threat, not a promise. Only losers, who know their need for reliance on strength beyond their own, can hear this announcement as good news. It offers them release from the tyranny of winners.

The second half of Mark's summary sentence expresses the response required by the news of God's rule. "Repent and believe in the gospel." What a terrible time winners have with that summons. A rich young man comes seeking eternal life, only to be told that he must become poor before he can receive it. Adults refuse to let children come to Jesus, only to be told that until they become like little children they can never enter the kingdom. Worldly values are set on their head. Jesus insists, "many that are first will be last, and the last first" (10:31).

Jesus is the Savior of all, but only seconds can receive him. It's no wonder that people seldom become Christians while they are in some sense a top banana. They need to be peeled of their primacy before the fruit of dependent faith can emerge. We have seen this illustrated repeatedly in in recent conversions of prominent Americans. Jimmy Carter's awakening of faith did not happen while governor of Georgia, but in the aftermath of a lost election. Eldridge Cleaver did not enter the kingdom while leading the black revolution, but while running from justice through Algeria. Charles Colson was not reborn while swimming in pools of presidential power, but after the bursting of Watergate drowned the deception of first-string self-sufficiency. The news of God's rule is good only to those who have been benched in repentance. They alone are able to trust this Savior of seconds.

What's more, the Savior came as a second himself. Mark identifies him as the Son of God twice in these first fifteen verses. But Jesus himself, as the story unfolds, insists on keeping his identity a secret. Being a servant himself, Mark could see the servanthood of Jesus and does not present him as the world's supreme prophet. Few of his teachings are recorded. Rather, the deeds of Jesus are paramount here. Mark shows him at work, freeing people from the tyrants that bind them. And Jesus explains his own role clearly in those memorable words Mark alone records: "For the Son of man . . . came not to be served but to serve; and to give his life as a ransom for many" (10:45).

You can trust a Savior who is willing to sacrifice his status and survival for your sake. You can yield first place to a Lord like that. Being second to him is not a put-down but an up-lift. You can serve a king like that, for in his kingdom a servant becomes prime minister.

The Service of Seconds

Entering the kingdom of God through the gate of penitent faith ushers us into a world of new values. We are free from the tyranny of victory. Here, winning is not the only thing. It's not anything. Serving is the only thing and that means a lot of losing. First and last, it means losing yourself. The teachings of Jesus which Mark does record press this point home repeatedly. Self denial, renunciation, bearing one's cross, and becoming servants to each other, these are the major themes.

That lesson has never been easily learned. James and John came to Jesus seeking positions of prestige in the kingdom. The others argue about which of them is greatest. The servant-Savior tells them how to achieve that status. "If anyone would be first, he must be last of all and servant of all (7:35). Mark could understand that. He knew that second-string status is neither an ego threat nor cause for self-depreciation. Self-worth is not destroyed. The exact opposite is true. The smallest act of assistance is now loaded with value and meaning. The more of a servant you are, the more like thre Master you become.

Does this speak to us who are ministers today? Does it suggest an increase or decrease in the use of titles like "Reverend" to identify us? Only God is to be reverenced! And how about our rush for doctorates of whatever kind? If letters are given in recognition of services rendered or used to designate equipment for special service, that's one thing. But if they become a tactic to elevate us from second to first-string status, that is quite another. Are we tempted by the leverage such titles provide to "lord it over" congregations and other ministries, as the Gentiles liked to do? Jesus said, "It shall not be so among you; but whoever would be great among you must be your servant and whoever would be first among you must be slave of all" (10:43-44).

It's encouraging to read that some are remembering the primacy of the secondary in ministry. Episcopal Bishop John Burt, himself a "right reverend," called on the clergy of his Ohio diocese to scrap the use of such titles. In support of his plea, he recalls our own denominational tradition. "I . . . have always envied the Lutherans in their custom of calling their minister pastor." In the kingdom of God, no titles are higher than those which designate service. Should we settle for anything less?

Does this mean no honor is to be given when honor is due? Has sacrifice no responding reward? Are human needs for esteem and recognition to be ignored? Jesus promised Peter that material and familial losses suffered "for my sake and for the gospel" would be restored "a hundred fold now in this time" (10:29-30). We can trust him to provide for our esteem needs as well.

The question is simply this, "What values are to be honored? Whom are we to esteem?" The answer is consistent in both the teaching and style of Jesus himself. Service is to be honored! Servants are to be esteemed! And in the long run they are.

Mark is an example of it. About A.D. 70 two men were at work on their separate tasks. One was Vespasian, a Roman general in charge of the occupation army in Judea. In A.D. 66, after a century of Roman rule, the Jews had successfully rebelled and taken control of Jerusalem. Two years later, Emperor Nero committed suicide and revolt broke out in Rome. General Vespasian was called to Rome, quenched the rebels and became head of the empire. He left his son Titus to deal with the Jewish question.

In the spring of 70, Titus rallied 80,000 troops around Jerusalem and cut off the food supply to the city. He captured those trying to escape and crucified up to five hundred of them daily on a forest of crosses around the city. Finally, he broke through the walls, desecrated the Temple and leveled it. Then in 71 he paraded his victorious army in a triumphant procession through the streets of Rome. You can hear them shouting: "We're No. 1. We're the Greatest." General Vespasian was clearly a first-stringer.

While all this was going on, a second-string servant was also in Rome, writing the story of Jesus. Nineteen centuries later only history buffs can tell you the name of that victor. But every Sunday school child can tell you the story of Jesus and the name of the servant who first wrote it. Yes, first wrote it! For biblical scholars have since discovered that Mark's gospel was not copied from those prominent evangelists, Apostle Matthew and Dr. Luke. Rather, they borrowed from Mark, using him as a primary source for their work. By 1976, at least one book of the Bible has been published in 1603 languages and dialects, including twenty-nine new ones last year. According to The American Bible Society, the first book printed in any new language is usually the Gospel of Mark.

So the second has become first. Honor has come to one who served as a second-string saint. May his tribe increase.

PAUL W. EGERTSON
St. Timothy Lutheran Church
Lakewood, California

AN EVEN GREATER PRESENCE
St. Philip and St. James, Apostles
May 1
John 14:8-14

What value is there in coming together to remember two obscure saints? Peter and Paul, Mary the Mother of our Lord, John to Baptist—these are persons who have left indelible marks on the Christian faith. But the total biographical information on Sts. Philip and James the Less would hardly fill the standard paragraphs in *Who's Who*. But maybe that's just the point. It's hard for us to identify with the super-heroes of the faith. Their examples seem so beyond us. But maybe these little-known saints are more our size. If they could make it into the gallery of the blessed one, so can we!

The Life of St. Philip

Look at St. Philip. We learn nothing about him in the synoptic gospels other than that he is listed among the twelve apostles. In St. Paul's Gospel he is mentioned several times, but what we learn about him isn't all that extraordinary. In fact, he strikes us as being very ordinary—just like us or people we have known.

We are told that the day after Jesus called Peter and Andrew to follow him, he "found Philip" and told him to follow too. We can guess from this that Philip was from Bethsaida in Galilee. He may have been one of those persons influenced by John the Baptist. That would explain why he responded to Jesus without hesitation. He had been prepared by John to watch for the coming of the Messiah. But that doesn't mean his knowledge of Jesus was perfect. When he went to tell his friend Nathanael, "We have found him of whom Moses in the law and also the prophets wrote," he identified this Messiah only as "Jesus of Nazareth, the son of Joseph."

This was not a very adventurous identification, although the restraint in Philip's missionary zeal has its value. He didn't force his discovery on unwilling ears or argue about it. He simply invited Nathanael to come and see for himself and then form an opinion. This kind of sober discretion figures again in the feeding of the five thousand. When Jesus saw the crowds he asked Philip, "How are we to buy bread, so that these people may eat?" Philip answered without much imagination, "Two hundred denarii would not buy enough bread for each of them to get a little." It took the more visionary Andrew to see the possibility in the five barley loaves and two fish which a small boy had in his lunch sack. That might not be much among so many, but Andrew thought something might be done with it as long as Jesus was in control of the situation.

Defective Spiritual Insight

In our gospel reading we get another glimpse of Philip's defective spiritual insight. The setting is the Upper Room in the night of Jesus' betrayal. He is telling the disciples about going away to prepare a place for them, and then coming back to take them with him, "that where I am you may be also." Thomas was confused and said he didn't know where Jesus was going, nor did he know the way. Jesus answered: "I am the way. . . . If you had known me, you would have known my Father also; henceforth you know him and have seen him."

Philip responds by asking Jesus to show them the Father. He had been with Jesus all this time, and he still could not make the identification between Jesus and the Father. Jesus challenges Philip and Thomas and all of us to believe his identity, preferably because we have known him as a person, but if not that, then at least because of what he has done.

Jesus' Departure to the Father

Perhaps it is of some consolation for us to realize that the original twelve, who were given such an important mission in spreading the good news of what God has done in Jesus, often moved on a superficial level. We aren't very quick to see possibilities or to demonstrate spiritual insight either. The disciples were rather slow in seeing the possibilities for mission in Jesus' ascension. But then, this discussion in the Upper Room was taking place before the resurrection.

For us, who live after that event, the words of Jesus in his "farewell address" are words of great comfort and promise. They assure us that the risen and exalted Christ continues in his church through his Spirit who brings the words and deeds of Jesus to our remembrance in each and every generation. The real meaning of Jesus' ascension is that he goes to the Father in order to be present in an even greater way through his Spirit in all times and in all places. As he comes to his church and is present in the words and deeds of his followers, "even greater works" will be performed. "Truly, truly, I say to you, he who believes in me will also do the works that I do; and greater works than these will he do, because I go to the Father." That is a staggering promise to his church.

Jesus' Presence in His Apostles

The Fourth Gospel operates with what we call an incarnational theology. The Word was made flesh and lived among us as a human being. The glory of God was gotten down on earthly streets and into earthly homes. In the Spirit of Jesus the church becomes the extension of the incarnation: the eyes of Christ for seeing, the heart of Christ for beating compassion, the arms of Christ for reaching out, the legs of Christ for getting up and going, the mouth of Christ for speaking good news. "Even greater works" are performed through this extended body of Christ than were performed by Jesus himself during his earthly ministry. For now Jesus has become a whole people. We lack no power to do these works, not because we have greater financial and technical resources in our highly organized, modern institutional church, but because we can ask anything we want in the name of the risen and exalted Christ, and he will do it.

The acts of the apostles provide case studies in the "greater works" which are performed by the church, and that's the real reason we make a special effort to remember and give thanks for even the least of the apostles. They had nothing more going for them than we do, who also have the Holy Spirit, the Word and the Sacraments. Let us remember that it took the resurrection and the gift of the Spirit to change that little band of disciples huddled together in the Upper Room into *real apostles,* ones who were sent out with the authority of Christ just as Christ himself was sent from the Father. The fourth century church historian, Eusebius, relates the tradition that even unadventuresome and unimaginative Philip preached the gospel in Asia Minor. Among other things, he is reported to have raised a dead man to life. The tradition of St. James the Less is even more spectacular.

The Life of St. James

James—the Less, or the younger—is most commonly held to the same person who is designated "James, the son of Alpheus" and "James, the brother of the Lord" ("brother" here probably meaning cousin). This James does not figure as prominently in the Gospel stories as James the Greater, the son of Zebedee and brother of John. But St. Paul tells us that this James was favored with a special appearance of the risen Lord before the ascension. This James was highly regarded by the people of Jerusalem and he became the bishop of the church in that city. He played a prominent role in the dispute between Peter and Paul over the inclusion of the Gentiles in the church. At what is called the Council of Jerusalem, where it was decided that the Gentiles who believed in Jesus need not be circumcized according to the Jewish rite, it was James who voiced the conclusion of the assembly, "it has seemed good to the Holy Spirit and to us."

Even Josephus, the Jewish historian, bears witness to James' good reputation and calls him "the most righteous of men." The story of the martyrdom of James, as told by Hegesippus in the latter part of the second century, has been preserved in Eusebius' *Church History*, and it goes this way.

James received the name, "the Just," because there were many men named James, but this James was regarded as a very holy person. He drank no wine or strong drink, ate no meat, did not cut his hair, did not anoint himself with oil, and did not bathe. He wore priestly robes and was permitted to enter the holy place. There he was found on his knees asking forgiveness on behalf of the people. He was on his knees so much that they became hard like a camel's.

Many people came to believe in Jesus through James, including some prominent persons. The scribes and the Pharisees were worried that the whole people would accept Jesus as the Christ. Perhaps not knowing James' position in the Christian community, they asked him to stand on the pinnacle of the Temple on the day of the Passover and try to dissuade the people from believing in Jesus.

So the scribes and the Pharisees placed James on the pinnacle of the Temple and cried up to him, "O Just One, in whom we ought all to put our trust, inasmuch as the people are gone astray after Jesus who was crucified, tell us what is the door of Jesus." And James replied with a loud voice, "Why do you ask me about the Son of Man, since he sits in heaven on the right hand of the Mighty Power, and shall come on the clouds of heaven?" In other words, James identified Jesus with the expected Messiah, the "Son of Man" who shall come with power and great glory as judge of all. As James gave his testimony the people started crying, "Hosanna to the Son of David." The scribes and the Pharisees had been outmaneuvered. Crying out, "The Just One has gone astray," they rushed up and pushed him off the pinnacle of the Temple. The fall did not kill him, so they began to stone him. As they did so, James prayed, "I beseech thee, O Lord God, Father, forgive them, for they know not what they do." One of the priests cried out, "Stop! What are you doing? The Just One is praying on your behalf." But one of the men, a fuller, took a stick with which he beat clothes, and brought it down on the head of James. Thus he was martyred, and they buried him at that spot beside the Temple.

The Works Go On

How did it happen that these two apostles came to be remembered on the same day? It is most likely because their relics were transferred to the Church of the Apostle in Rome, which was completed in A.D. 563, and which was originally dedicated on May 1 in honor of Sts. Philip and James in particular. In these two very different men, who are not unlike other people we have known, and who may be very much like ourselves, the works of Christ were carried on. Christ's work went on because these men lived in the confidence that Jesus, their master and friend, who had been crucified, was raised from the dead by the glory of the Father and now lives and reigns with him, in the unity of the Spirit, forever and ever. The story of Jesus was not over with the end of the earthly ministry. It went on in the apostolic ministry and it continues even now in our ministry. It can be carried on even by the least of us. We have Jesus' Word; we have his Sacrament. We can pray too, and so we have his power to enable us to do whatever needs to be done in his name, and to do works which are even greater than he did.

FRANK C. SENN
Fenner Memorial Lutheran Church
Louisville, Kentucky

SPIRITED COURTESY

The Visitation
May 31
Luke 1:39-47

Can you imagine a more Spirit-filled case of courtesy in which the genuine love of which the Apostle Paul speaks in today's second reading, than that between the two noble women of today's text? This exchange of greeting between Elizabeth, the mother of John the Baptizer and Mary, the Mother of Our Lord, shows us two pious women putting into practice what the Apostle urges on us all. Let us consider the Apostle's instruction and the story of the visit of these two women that we ourselves may be stirred to follow them in that blessed faith, which is chastity before God, and in that genuine love, which is courtesy toward others. May the "Spirited Courtesy" displayed between these two women become common among us.

The Common, Not the Exceptional, Case of Love

Let us not turn these women into a pair of plastic saints and the scene of their visit into a never-never land. Consider, rather, what the Apostle Paul teaches us in the reading today about genuine love. Our love is not to be an imitation, a simulation game, turning Christian love into something unlike love. Genuine love abhors the evil as evil; it clings to the good as good. And yet, it is no cold, steely, and frigid perception of the good and the evil in ourselves or in others that always distances itself from the other. Rather, it is a love marked by affection; it looks at the other to bestow honor first upon the other. Genuine love has a way of presenting itself by bowing in honor to the other—even though the external act of bowing (as the partners in a formal dance or the square dance are trained to do) may not be present. The mind of this love has the modesty of a gracious giver, one who wills to honor the other.

The Apostle exhorts us to be zealous in this courteous love. We are not dogs, trained to jump through the hoop on command; rather, we are servants of the Lord, and made so by the generous service the Lord himself has rendered to us. Hence, we are to continue to be served by him to the end that the service with which we are served is the vitality that keeps us energetic in fervor of the spirit to serve God in our work. The creating and giving God who serves us is neither lazy nor slothful in his business. Therefore, we do not adopt the mentality of cool indifference about our service; our mind is to mind the work with the intensity of God.

Joyful in Hope

It would be an error for us to think that such zeal must become grim and stolid, gritting its teeth and setting its jaw against impending failure. The Apostle speaks rather of a lively and buoyant hope, a hope that nurtures joy. Such joy is known by the old and barren Elizabeth as she awaited the birth of that which was already forming in her, the kind of joy Mary expresses in her song.

Hence, when tribulations knock you about, perhaps the way an expectant mother would know the distress in her body as the chemistry and shape of it change, be patient and durable. Wait, as you lie tucked down under God's mighty hand. And while you wait, persist ready in prayer. With hearts quick to trust the kind of pity of your heavenly Father, cling to him who loves to have you call on him. Let your hearts leap instantly and constantly to that one from whom your life comes.

Bless; Don't Curse

Faith toward God does not separate one from others in need. Rather, it drives one into the courtesies with others. Thus, the Apostle makes the common needs of the saints something to which we give diligent attention. Hospitality, which is the name of this courtesy, is to be pursued with the attention of a host who wants guests to be in comfort and in joy.

For some people prayer goes in reverse. They use God's name, but they use it to invoke the power of death and destruction on others. They may call upon God, but they ask him to damn, not bless. You, for your part, bless. Do not curse those who seek your harm.

To bless is also to be a blessing. You not only say the good; you live the good for the others. Give yourselves to the partnership with lowly people and the lowly tasks. Rather than having an over-inflated opinion of yourself, give attention to bring your high place and your high gifts to the service of lowly things and lowly people.

Take Elizabeth, for Example

In a society where priests were an honored and select people, Elizabeth had the high position of being the wife of a priest. In a society where old age was honored, Elizabeth, an old woman, was held in high regard. In a society which considered barrenness a curse, Elizabeth was a barren woman. Now, far beyond the normal child-bearing years, Elizabeth was expecting a child. And what a child! None would be greater in the kingdom of heaven. In a society and time when much of the piety was for profit or for praise, Elizabeth was (with her husband) a pious woman of prayer. When even her husband could not overcome his suspicion of the word of God about the birth of the son, Elizabeth was courageous enough to take all contradictions to that word captive to it and await the son.

A noble, well-married old woman whose life of prayer and faithfulness had been chastened with the most public and painful disappointment of barrenness, Elizabeth was now awaiting the birth of the child who might very well be the standard of all good and pious humans. Elizabeth does not talk like a silly, bitter old woman, nor like a haughty and proud woman, finally finding her self-fulfillment. She neither sneers nor snorts at Mary, this young, lowly peasant woman who is coming to her with child, even though she is not yet married.

Rather, from Elizabeth's mouth there pours forth the most courteous and grave blessing, a most solemn announcement, "Blessed are you among women, and blessed is the fruit of your womb." Though she was a woman of high estate, Elizabeth's soul bursts out with awe, "Why is it granted to me that the mother of my Lord should come to me?" She who was high bows herself down in courtesy before this woman of lowly estate.

Elizabeth's courteous treatment of the young virgin mother-to-be has another benefit: she is a courteous servant for you today who hear this story. In the mouth of this pious old woman there is truth to guide and direct you who hear this text. She describes how the fetus in her womb "leaped for joy" at the greeting of Mary. True blessedness, she makes clear, is not and was not the biological connection of Mary with the Son to be born of her; it was, and is, rather the faith that trusts the promising and saving word of God to be fulfilled in the recipient of that promise. "Blessed is she who believed that there would be fulfillment of what was spoken to her from the Lord."

Take Mary as Another Example

And in that other lady, the Blessed Virgin Mary, there is the same chastity toward God and the same courtesy toward the other. Here is no false modesty seeking to stroke itself into importance by a show of self-deprecation. Neither is there the self-degeneration of pride. In Mary there is the innocent delight that grows from faith. She relaxes in the work that God is doing in her, to her, and through her. She receives the word that brings the work of God for her and for us. Hence, Mary breaks forth in sheer delight at the honorable greeting, for she enjoys the work of God as if—indeed more than if—it were her own work. No alloy of pride, no confusion from shame mars that chastity. Only delight marks her response. She, the lowly handmaid of the Lord, magnifies the mercy of God.

The faith of Mary corresponds in a most appropriate way to the perfect faithfulness of God. God's fidelity in keeping promises impels him to make the move toward the lowliness of the birth of his Son. In stooping so far down in his redeeming courtesy toward us his creatures, God comes to the lowly Mary; she meets him with fidelity. And Mary's fidelity toward that donating God makes open the way for God faithfully to bless each of you and all of you today. God did his work in and through her, not only for her benefit, but also for ours.

What of Our Chastity and Courtesy?

We can trade places with neither Elizabeth nor Mary. Neither can we trade places with our parents and children, our fellow-members in God's family, not our neighbors. By the spontaneity and freedom of his will, God has placed us not only inside our skin but also in an irreversible position with certain other people. For hearts that cannot trust God and for lives that live not in the certainty of his pleasure but only under the fear that life will be snatched away from them, there can be no courtesy toward the other; only calculation. There can be no courtesy toward the other because there is no chastity in the heart toward God; only mistrust.

These women, Elizabeth and Mary, are flesh and blood examples of how God's Spirit takes a word of promise from God, puts flesh and blood into that promise by the coming of Jesus Christ, and with that word, cleanses and purifies the heart of faith. Jesus Christ in the heart of faith is our chastity before God. Not cursed but blessed is every man, woman, and child who believes that God fulfills the promise he has spoken to us. Such a chaste heart and soul, certain of its vitality in God's gracious promise, is the heart that loves genuinely, not with simulation games of love. Its courtesy toward the other is spirited by that Lord Jesus who, being sinned against, came down in lowliness to stoop under, pick up, and serve with salvation all who trust in him.

Today is the celebration of Mary's "Visitation" to Elizabeth. They came to look at each other and thereby to see the works of God. With the chaste eyes of faith, Elizabeth, by the word of God, honors the lowly Mary; with the chaste eyes of faith, Mary, by the word of God, magnifies the Lord and rejoices in God, her Savior. With Jesus Christ as the mediatorial center between God and you, let your faith trust that word of blessing. And, as you live with each other, let the chastity in your hearts mold your courtesy toward the other. In that way, you see God as larger in his grace when you look at each other. Thus, the look that you give each other will be the donation of honor to each other, as God in Christ Jesus has honored you.

KENNETH F. KORBY
Valparaiso University
Valparaiso, Indiana

A GREAT CHRISTIAN
St. Barnabas, Apostle
June 11
Acts 11:19-30; 13:1-3

It isn't easy to play second fiddle. It's doubly difficult if the man in the first violinist's chair is someone you have befriended and helped so that he could become a member of the orchestra. Jealousy finds a place in almost every human heart, even in the hearts of those who are good Christians.

Yet our worship this morning honors a man who underwent such a temptation and apparently emerged unscathed. Today we honor St. Barnabas, one of the early leaders of the Christian church. It was Barnabas who befriended Paul when others were afraid of this persecutor-turned-convert. It was Barnabas who brought Paul to the attention of the church at Jerusalem and again at Antioch. It was Barnabas who set out on a missionary journey with Paul as his assistant and soon found it was to be Paul and Barnabas, not Barnabas and Paul. Indeed so complete was the eclipse that soon this great Christian disappears from the Book of Acts and Paul takes over the spotlight completely.

It is not my intention to try to rescue Barnabas from obscurity or to leave the impression that history has been unkind to him. Rather I think we should see in Barnabas a man who may not have been a great leader but who certainly was a great Christian. And in these days when Christians are often criticized and exposed as poor examples of their faith, it is a good time to see the opposite, a good time to listen to the story of a great Christian.

There are three simple characteristics mentioned about Barnabas. He was a good man, a man full of the Holy Spirit, a man of faith. Those are fine characteristics and worth further thought.

A Good Man

Those are words that we usually hear at someone's funeral. He was a good man. She was a good woman. But we don't mention them too often when speaking about a living individual. Somehow, to call a person "good" is to condemn them to dullness and anonymity. It's the villain who attracts our attention. The woman who kicks over the traces gets her name in the newspaper. The teenager who is a bit on the wild side becomes the school hero or heroine.

Yet it is goodness that God seeks in this world. He has rescued us from sin so that we might be good people. "Blessed is the man who fears the Lord, who greatly delights in his commandments," says the psalm for today. And certainly this world needs more good people. We need people who are honest and charitable and loving. We need good people in politics, in business, in labor unions, yes, even in the church. I know that God forgives sinners. The thieves, the prostitutes, the jailbirds are welcome in the kingdom of God. But God calls them and us to righteousness, to goodness.

The word "good" certainly describes Barnabas. We don't know how or when he became a Christian. Some have thought he was one of those seventy disciples of Jesus that the gospels mention. Others, noting that he came from Cyprus, think he was a man who was converted at Pentecost. But one thing we know. Very early in the history of the church Barnabas sold a field and gave the money to be used to care for the poor. And every mention of his name after that tells us that he was a man of integrity, a man trusted by every section of the early church. He was a good man.

But there is another meaning to the term "goodness." It also means someone who is a good workman, good at whatever he does. And the title fits Barnabas. For he did whatever he was called on to do and he did it with real efficiency. It was Barnabas who spoke up for Paul when the rest of the Christian leaders were fraid of this new convert. It was Barnabas who was chosen to go from Jerusalem to Antioch to see what was happening there and he had the good sense once again to summon Paul to help him. It was Barnabas who took a gift from Antioch to Jerusalem and when it was decided at Antioch to send out missionaries to the Gentiles, Barnabas again was chosen for the task. No wonder this man, whose name originally was Joseph, received the name that he bore, for Barnabas means son of encouragement or comfort. This man was a good man, good at doing the Lord's work.

And God needs men and women like that. Sometimes we get the notion that God only wants the simpletons and the weak brothers and sisters in the church. And it is true that God uses some dull tools at times. Peter Marshall in a sermon once said that the only disciple human wisdom would have chosen would have been Judas; the rest were flawed and weak. But that's not all the picture.

After all, Paul was the most productive of the Apostles, and he was also the most gifted. The great leaders of the church have not been dunderheads. There is no prize for inefficiency or stupidity. God can use the ten-talent people too. The finest art, the best science, are useful to him. He always wants people like Barnabas, good men and women in his kingdom. If God has given you a talent, use it in his service.

Full of the Holy Spirit

But there is often a flaw in the actions of good people, efficient people. Because they are capable, they often think they don't need any outside help. If you're smart or rich or moral, you are tempted to rely on your own strength. "I can handle this job all by myself," people think, and that's asking for trouble. That's why we need to note what is said about this great Christian, Barnabas. He was a man "full of the Holy Spirit." **Perhaps it was Barnabas who taught Paul to say, "I worked harder than any of them, though it was not I, but the grace of God which is with me" (1 Cor. 15:10).**

The truth is that Christians are very weak when they stand alone. The Bible warns us against thinking that we can stand against the temptations of this world. Every one of us is a pushover for Satan if we try to beat him by good resolutions or clever human actions. Those old adversaries, the world, the flesh and the devil, always will defeat us. We need the Spirit of God in our lives. We need to rely on God's power. To be filled with the Holy Spirit is to be prepared for the attacks of the enemy.

Martin Luther was once asked where he would be if the princes and the German leaders deserted him. He answered, "Right where I was from the beginning, in the hands of God." Barnabas must have known that power too. After all, it took courage to sponsor Paul when everyone was afraid of him. It took courage to leave Jerusalem for work in Antioch among the Gentiles. It took even more courage to launch out on that first missionary journey, during which the missionaries were threatened by a sorcerer at Cyprus, and Paul was stoned at Lystra.

But Barnabas had strength in the midst of all this. He was full of the Holy Spirit. God had filled his heart and life. And every Christian needs to follow his example. We may not have to go off on a missionary journey and nobody may be threatening to persecute us, but we will not win even the little battles of life if we try to do it all alone. Barnabas was a great Christian because he had what makes a Christian great—God's Holy Spirit to guide and strengthen him.

A Man of Faith

The last descriptive term seems like an anticlimax. We are told that Barnabas was a man of faith. After being told that he was full of the Holy Spirit, shouldn't that be enough? In one sense perhaps, yes. But faith is a great Bible word and dare not be overlooked. For here it seems to tell us that Barnabas believed in something. In those early years when the good news of the gospel was both news and new, it was important to know that this great Christian was not a man filled with doubts and controversies. He had faith. While we don't get any creedal statement by Barnabas, it is interesting to note that it was at Antioch where Barnabas and Paul were teaching that the disciples were first called Christians.

And that is significant. For Christianity is a faith founded on Christ. Christianity is the teaching that God, out of love for human beings, sent his son into the world to live and die and rise from the dead so that we might have life now and for eternity. Our religion isn't a fine whirl of words. It's faith in what God has done. Sometimes people want us to give up all our doctrine and be satisfied with some moral teachings. "Let the doctrine go. Keep the Christian ethic," an English philosopher said a few years ago. But that can't be. Like Barnabas, we have a faith. We believe in something or rather in someone. In the words of an old hymn,

> I know whom I believe in,
> I know what firm abides,
> When all around me fading
> Away like vapor glides.
> I know what lasts forever,
> When all things shake and fall,
> When wit the wise forsaketh,
> And craft doth craft forestall.

Barnabas never heard that hymn. But I'm sure it expresses his feeling. He didn't even have the New Testament as we do today. But he was a man of faith. And Christianity is a religion of faith. You and I can marvel that the message which he and Paul preached is still the heart of our message today. It is still our faith. And we rejoice in it.

Barnabas Wasn't Perfect

I should stop here, for we have said all that our brief text says about Barnabas. But it would be an injustice to the man himself to omit one more truth this morning. Barnabas was a great Christian. But he wasn't perfect. He deserted his gentile friends on one occasion and had to be rebuked by Paul. Worse than that, he and Paul got into a quarrel and had to divide their missionary efforts. The quarrel was a very human one. On the first missionary journey they took along a young man, John Mark, who was a relative of Barnabas. For some reason, Mark didn't finish that journey but deserted and went home. So, when the second journey was proposed, Paul wanted to leave Mark at home, but Barnabas wanted to give him another chance. And the quarrel grew so bitter that the missionaries separated and each went his separate way.

Now why bring that up? No one expects Barnabas to be perfect, but why mention it after all these years? For a very good reason. Human beings tend to glorify their leaders. And then they very upset when the leader proves to have feet of clay. Christians are very susceptible to that. We find someone whom we think is a great Christian and then we are all upset when some weakness is exposed. So the story of Barnabas is important to us. He was a great Christian. But he wasn't perfect. And we shouldn't be shocked when someone we respect proves to be less than perfect. Don't quit the church if the pastor loses his temper or a seemingly fine woman runs away with her next-door neighbor.

For there is really only one great Christian—Jesus Christ. He is the one sinless one, the good man, the one filled with the Holy Spirit, the man of faith. All the rest of us, Barnabas included, are simply pale imitations of him. All the rest follow with halting steps the path where Jesus walked.

And yet, though the light from Jesus puts everything else into darkness, it is a good thing from time to time to remember the great Christians, the great men and women who have lived before us. Barnabas was one of them. You and I have the gospel, humanly speaking, because of godly human beings like Barnabas. Only God can reward him for his faithfulness, but let us honor him today.

W. A. POOVEY
Dubuque, Iowa

LASTING MIDSUMMER JOYS
The Nativity of St. John the Baptizer
June 24
Luke 1:57-67 (68-80)

Midsummer is a glowing time of the year. The smiles of life burst into hearty laughter. The earth is beautiful: "What is so rare as a day in June? Then—if ever—come perfect days." The very air is fragrant with enchantment: fairies and brownies disport themselves in the greenwood—note, for instance, "A Midsummer Night's Dream" by Shakespeare. Midsummer is rich in memories, too. It is a festive day in many, many parts of the world—such as Quebec—Mexico—Sweden—as well as in many American communities.

In the Church Year, Midsummer Day—June 24—is the *Festival of the Birth—the Nativity of St. John the Baptizer.*

It was St. Augustine who pointed out that John's life motto (John 3:30): "He must increase but I must decrease," is written right on the calendar in our part of the world—the days are longest at the summer solstice, the Festival of the Birth of John (born six months before Jesus), and then grow shorter till Christmas, December 25, the Festival of the Birth of Our Lord—whereupon light again increases and darkness decreases.

John is a fascinating, mysterious figure: His aloneness in the hot, dusty desert—fatherless, motherless, sisterless, brotherless; his food—grasshoppers and wild honey; his drink—Adam's ale (water); his clothing—coarse camel's hair and a leather belt; his shelter—a cave; his transportation—the apostles' horses (his own two sturdy legs); his stern message—impending judgment.

John had taken a life-long Nazirite vow, like Samson and Samuel, never to have a haircut, never to touch a dead or unclean thing, never to touch alcoholic beverage—total separation—regardless of the cost—from the life-style of the heathen idol-worshipers who surrounded him.

DID YOU KNOW . . . that John the Baptist is mentioned 100 times in the New Testament, more than any other person except Jesus, Peter, and Paul?

. . . that he is the last of the Old Testament prophets (who dressed like an Old Testament prophet—2 Kings 1:8, Zech. 13:4) after the prophetic voice had been silent for 14 generations or 420 years?

. . . that he is the first of the New Testament evangelists?

... that all four of the Gospel writers, Matthew, Mark, Luke, and John, begin the story of the Gospel with the story of John the Baptist?

... that John is the clasp which binds the two Testaments—the Old Testament and the New Testament—together?

... that he is the morning star, penciled out quickly by the rising Sun?

... that he is the herald who rides ahead on horseback into the village and tells the people: "Get your homes and your highways cleaned up and ready, for the King is coming this way!"?

... that there is more art work—paintings, statues, mosaics—of John the Baptizer than of any other person in history outside of Mary and Jesus?

... that John occupies the place of great honor in the Eastern Orthodox Church, pictured on the panel next to Jesus on one side with Mary the Lord's mother on the other side?

... that John was very popular in the medieval monasteries with their stress on the disciplines?

John is so very often pictured as stern, austere, even emaciated. How can this earnest preacher of the fire of judgment—of turning away from sin—possibly fit in with the midsummer mood of gaiety?

I believe the artists have pictured John as too sad a man.

Let's look at his life as a picture of *Lasting Midsummer Joy.* Here we have another of the Bible's rich paradoxes.

Behold John the Joy-Bringer

In anticipation of his birth:

There is a note of joy sounded right away in the Gospel account of John the Baptizer. When in the temple the angel Gabriel announces to father Zechariah that he and Elizabeth are to have a son, the angel says (Luke 1:14): "You shall have *joy* and *gladness* and *many* shall *rejoice* at his birth." "You"—John was a prayed for, longed for child; therefore, a great joy would come to the parents. "Many"—like a stone dropped in the middle of a pool which forms ever-widening circles—John will bring joy to relatives, to friends—and to the nation, and to all humanity, in all succeeding ages.

At his arrival: His birth brought joy.

When this triple-miracle boy was born to this childless couple now well beyond the normal age of having children (and it was predicted before his birth that it would be a male child), we are told (Luke 1:58): "And mother Elizabeth's neighbors and relatives heard how the Lord had showed great mercy on her; and they rejoiced with her." The neighbors and musicians stood by the house and struck up joyous music as soon as they got the good news of his birth.

Elizabeth and Zechariah were overjoyed. At the circumcision on the eighth day, as Zechariah names his son "John" in obedience to what Gabriel had told him, Zechariah's tongue is loosed and his very first act is to burst into a joyous paean known as the "Benedictus" (Luke 1:68-79). The "Benedictus" is a remarkable song which contains in embryo the whole life and ministry of John.

There is joy in his possibilities:

A child—and doubly so this child—is a bundle of infinite possibilities. A baby is a message from God that he is not yet discouraged with the human race. "What shall this child be?" all rightfully ask in wonder.

John the Joy-Possessor

It is a law of life that the giver of joy is also the possessor of joy—joy is like jam: you can't spread it without getting some on yourself.

The joy of godly parents:

The home of Zechariah and Elizabeth was the kind out of which God's great ones come. Elizabeth was a wonderful mother (in the Catholic church she is the patron saint of mothers), who knew the secret of Christian assurance (Luke 1:45). He had a tremendous father, Zechariah. His folks belonged to the "quiet of the land" who were eagerly awaiting the Messiah. It was a home abounding in prayer, music, poetry, and friendly hospitality.

The joy of a great pardon:

He knew his own—and mankind's—illness—and the remedy. In a hospital a person may lie for a couple of weeks—not well, increasingly uptight, not knowing what is wrong. Then one morning the doctor comes in smiling and says: "Rejoice; I've been studying the tests and the x-rays and I've found out what's causing your illness. Furthermore, I know the remedy (surgery, medication, therapy) which will fix you up so you'll be better than new." Such was the "good news" (Luke 3:18) John preached. For John knew that the disease of mankind which creates alienation, bondage, and death is sin. In Byzantine art John is always pictured with a scroll on which is written: "Repent, for the kingdom of heaven is at hand" (Matt. 3:2).

Sin is a cancer in the bloodstream of the world and it must have a blood remedy. So in his swan song as the first of the New Testament evangelists, John points to Christ and says: "Behold, the Lamb of God!" (John 1:29, 36). In Western art John is always pictured with a scroll which reads: "Behold the Lamb of God!"—which means that in some amazing way, known fully only to God, Christ came and took our place, lived a perfect life for us, died for us, rose again for us, set us free. John knew this by personal experience for himself—and knew that this was the only answer for all mankind.

He knew the joy of a clean conscience. I believe John in the dungeon was a happier man than superstitious, cowardly, fear-ridden, licentious Herod in the palace. He also knew the joy of being a truly free man—not enslaved by his appetites—unaddicted—the master of his body.

The joy of a glad presence:

John searched the depths of the Scriptures. He was steeped in Isaiah, Jeremiah, Malachi particularly—no doubt knew these books by heart, and had probably spent a third of the night meditating upon them and the Law during the years he studied in the Essene monastery.

John prayed—and taught his disciples to pray (Luke 11:1). He knew the joy of solitude. He could say with the poet: "My mind to me a Kingdom is, such present joys therein I find that it excels all other bliss that earth affords or grows by kind."

His friends were also friends of God. Simon, Andrew, James, John, Philip—these young men mentioned in John 1 were very likely John's disciples before they became disciples of Christ. Thus John knew the joys of bracing fellowship with like-minded young men united in a great overtowering purpose—who strengthened his hand in God.

The joy of a growing purpose:

Jean Paul Sartre, the atheistic existentialist, said: "Life adds up to zero—it has no meaning, no purpose—a nightmare between two nothings." And life *is* grim—apart from God. But with God, in fellowship with him, building his eternal Kingdom, it is full of meaning, adventure, excitement—and the living hope.

In fact, when Mary came to visit Elizabeth, the unborn John under Elizabeth's heart "leaped for joy" (Luke 1:44) in his first witness to Christ.

John was called to a tremendous task. He was a young man "sent from God" to prepare the way of the Lord. He had a magnificent obsession. He had the joy of giving himself totally for—even suffering for—a cause bigger than himself, and seeing that cause go forward.

And John's motto was: "Christ must grow greater and greater and I less and less" (John 3:30 Phillips). John knew the joy of all-out commitment. So many folks who claim to be Christ's followers dissipate their time and energy commuting between two worlds—and lose the real joy of the Christian life.

Happiness is a will-o'-the-wisp which eludes us when it is exclusively pursued. When we live for God and for others, it steals upon us unawares. John says (in John 3:29)—"I am the best man"—and having brought Christ the Bridegroom and his Church the Bride together—he affirms—"my joy is now full, complete." There is no joy in life comparable to the joy of being the instrument to bring people to know Jesus Christ.

The joy of gentle pleasures:

John was an outdoor man, bronzed by the wilderness sun and wind. His illustrations are all of outdoor life: the winnowing of grain, the building of a road, the woodsman cutting down a tree, the viper fleeing before the burning stubble. He knew the special enjoyment of nature which is given to the pure in heart.

The joy of a glorious prospect:

Today, in eternity, would you rather be weak and wicked King Herod or John the Baptist? John was fearless—for he knew God had his heart, hence he wasn't so worried about his neck. John, having preached nine months and having been imprisoned a year, lost his head on a platter at Herod's birthday party at age 32. But the pain and discomfort of prison faded in the light of his future glorious destiny. He could say with Paul: "I reckon the suffering of this present time is not worthy to be compared with the splendor ahead" (Rom. 8:18). In John 3:31-36 (which I believe are the thoughts of John the Baptizer as he is coming to the close of a brief, tempestuous ministry) we read: "He who believes in the Son has eternal life"—as a present possession. (Really the only thing that made John sad was when people failed to receive his witness to Christ. Cf. John 3:32.)

Are These Joys of Life for Us?

We have a super-abundance of "things." All around us we see people engaged in a frenetic search for pleasure—combined with much unhappiness.

Do we have the joy of a *happy home life?* If not, how can we make a positive contribution to joy in whatver situation we are placed? Do we have the joy of *knowing the heart of life*—the forgiveness of sins? Do we have the joy of *being free persons in Christ?* Do we have the joy of daily *fellowship with God* in worship—in his Word—in prayer? Do we have the joy of *fellowship with God's people*—not on the edge, but in the heart of it? Do we have Christian joy in the world about us: a sunrise, a sunset, a bird, a flower, a baby's smile? Do we have the joy of an *all-out commitment to a great purpose*—living to build God's eternal kingdom? Do we have the joy of an *assured and glorious future?*

May God give you and me in abundance *lasting Midsummer joys!*

WILTON E. BERGSTRAND
Holy Trinity Lutheran Church
Jamestown, New York

CAUGHT IN THE EMBRACE
St. Peter and St. Paul, Apostles
June 29
1 Corinthians 3:16-23

One must wonder about the economy of the ancient fathers in appointing days for the remembrance of the great heroes of the faith. Today we celebrate the life and witness of those two giants of the apostolic church, Peter and Paul. But just why these two Spirit-filled men share a single day of celebration while others about whom we know very little—like Matthias—get a day all to themselves, is a mystery. At any rate, since these two are to be celebrated on this day, we are given opportunity to look at them separately and together as the principal human architects of a church that is at once "catholic" and "evangelical."

Two Distinct Personalities

A search of the Gospels and the book of Acts, and of the writings that the church identifies with Peter and Paul reveals some startling differences. Peter emerges from the pages of the sacred Scripture as the impetuous, vacillating champion of his Lord, whom he identified as "the Christ, the Son of the living God." Probably thousands of sermons have referred to those well-known characteristics of his personality that make Peter the disciple with whom we can most easily identify. We are all too familiar with the ups-and-downs of the life of faith. We all know what it's like to be silent when we should have spoken, and what it's like to speak up, only to say the wrong thing. We identify well with Peter—most of us do, at least.

Paul, on the other hand, has a more elusive personality to identify with, for most of us. In our age of easy conformity Paul's white-hot, passionate, singlemindedness comes off as sheer fanaticism. We tend to avoid the kind of confrontational style of Paul. We are more inclined toward gentle persuasion and sweet reasonableness, and less inclined to plunge head-on into a reckless pursuit of the mission we share with him. And yet, who among us has not felt his heart burn within him when Paul's rhapsodic eloquence penetrates the crust of our twentieth century sophistication, our frequent willingness to avoid conflict rather than meeting sin and injustice with judgment and mercy.

One Common Center

It is easy to conclude that there are decided differences between Peter and Paul—differences that at least once broke out in an emotionally-charged confrontation. Read the second chapter of Paul's letter to the Galatians for the details if you have a chance, and you will discover that Paul's less-than-temperate determination to be about his mission to the gentiles caused him to confront Peter's weakness to his face.

But we miss the point by a mile if we confine ourselves to a mere examination of surface differences—the quirks and idiosyncracies of personality—that too often are accepted as the earmarks of identity. And that is a good part of the church's problem in nearly every generation. It was true at Corinth, and it's true today. We are inclined to evaluate the externals so carefully that we never perceive, or appreciate, or affirm what is at the center. It is not at the edges of personality—either of the individual person or of the corporate personality of a community—that we discover the meaning or motive. It is at the center of the being that we discover what makes a person or a church tick.

Despite their great differences in direction, in style, in personality—Peter and Paul shared a luminous, common, constant center—Jesus Christ. Each of them had his unique history. Each of them had his unique history in Christ. Their experience of their Lord was vastly different—but in each experience the apostle was summoned out of the human clay to move among Christ's people with authority, with grace, with power, and with love. These two men from different backgrounds, different life experience, were caught in the embrace of a loving Father, who not only caught them up, but called and commissioned them for ministry among his people.

Diversity in the Ancient Church

That ministry, given by the church's Lord to those apostles, included the call to the emerging churches to recognize and celebrate the unity of the Spirit in the midst of the obvious diversity that was present among them. It is difficult for us even to imagine the wide variety of people who had been assembled by the Holy Spirit in the churches around the Mediterranean in the first century. Looking back, as we must, from what we believe to be a pluralistic twentieth century to those ancient days, we have trouble comprehending just how diverse the church must have been in Corinth, for instance. We know that the church included some of that city's important leaders. At the same time, since most of the people of the ancient world lived in the underculture of slavery, many of the members of the Corinthian church were slaves. There was a Jewish community in Corinth, and there were people from that tradition who had been joined to this body as well.

There were differences in language, no doubt, since Corinth was a commercial crossroads of the ancient world. There were differences in national and ethnic background, differences in economic status, differences in cultural perceptions and values—and even differences among them in the cultic expression of their new-found religion. But the plea of the apostle is for that homogeneous mix of Christians to look beyond the obvious diversity among them to the central power of God that unites them. There is a word of warning—"Do you not know that you are God's temple and that God's Spirit dwells in you? If any one destroys God's temple, God will destroy him. For God's temple is holy, and that temple you are." You are joined together in a fellowship created by the Spirit of God—and in what God joins together man must not cause division.

Paul refers to three of the great evangelist-preachers who traveled that ancient world, and the implication is that despite all the differences you might detect in style, in surface characteristics—yet the message of them all is the same, "All things are yours, and you are Christ's and Christ is God's." You have been caught in the embrace of a loving Father together with the whole of the church throughout the world. And that Father who has embraced you does not seek to squeeze you into a narrow conformity of style, or of perception, or of personality. Rather, let the church with all its wide range of style and interest and expression bear witness to the creative power of God. Let the differences among you signify the greatness of God's power who can reach through individual differences to accomplish his will and work—and through those same differences give the variegated, diverse—and yet unified witness to the heart of it all—the faith of the church in its Lord and Savior, Jesus Christ.

Pressure for Uniformity

We live in a day when there is great pressure for uniformity all around us. How our culture enjoys the tidiness and neatness of "a place for everything and everything in its place!" How immense is the pressure for conformity among our young people! Be like everyone else. Don't stand out in the crowd. Choose your clothes from the same fashion catalog. Style your hair according to the accepted pattern. Be found in the right company of friends. And it's not only the young people, is it? All of us are a little fearful about daring to be different. Even the church sometimes seeks to jam people into the convenient pigeonholes of programs organized by age groups or interest groups. Business and industry look with suspicion upon the oddball—the one whose life-style is different. The collective eyebrows of the neighborhood are raised when a family moves in that seems "different." And you and I need to be reminded that when those surface differences are discovered among those with whom we share a sense of community, it's time to get past that "different" surface and begin to explore the center.

The Christian congregation in the setting of 20th century North America may not have the degree of differences that were mixed together in that church at Corinth. But there is no question that we do have our differences. Some years ago I served a congregation in a small town. In that congregation among those marvelous people of God, there were two men who were close and fast friends. Bill was a rising executive in one of the great industrial corporations in our country. Marvin was a part-time farmer and rural mail carrier who grew up in that somewhat simpler, small-town environment. Their life-styles were quite different. Their personalities were quite different. Bill was a gregarious, noisy, "can-do" rising executive-type. Marvin was subdued, serious and conservative in his life-style. But there was a genuine, warm, rich friendship between these two. In their widely different manners, it was hard to understand how they could be so close to each other—except for the center of each of them. The center was the Lord Jesus Christ. They shared a common commitment to Christ, a common urgency about Christ's mission, a common love for Christ's church. Except for that common strand of commitment, they might never have come to know—and be enriched by—each other. Diverse? Oh, yes they were! But unified? Indeed! They had discovered something about one another that the church must continue to discover at every opportunity. They had discovered that all of us have been caught in the embrace of a loving God.

Unity Within Diversity

It's time for us to set aside those neat little inventions of human wisdom that make us want to separate ourselves from those others who aren't like us at all—and begin to get to know one another for what we are—gifts of God to one another. We are all "fearfully and wonderfully made" by God. His unending creativity has fashioned us as distinct and different individuals. But with all of our apparent diversity, God has called us together to be his temple in this place—a living temple made up of unique and distinct people, yet filled with his grace so that we might see the unity we have in Christ.

Not long ago I visited a church that had a banner hanging in the confirmation class meeting room that read, "In essential things unity; in nonessential things freedom; in all things love." This slogan describes in a few words the kind of church the Lord was building through these two giants of the faith, Peter and Paul. It is a church that is "catholic"—that finds its core and center in Jesus Christ, and in its clear witness to him as Savior and Lord. Jesus Christ has been at the heart and center of the catholic church everywhere and at all times. At the same time, the church is "evangelical"—it is founded in the freedom of the Gospel—the freedom that continually searches for creative expression of its life and hope in every age. And that means that the church's method may change, personalities will come and go, style and manner may be altered to meet new challenges and opportunities, but at the heart will always be a common witness to the church's uncommon Lord.

He has called us together so he can share his gifts with us—gifts of forgiveness, life, salvation. And in those gifts we have the joy of discovery—we discover that you and I are caught in his embrace just as we are, possessing all the gifts he has given us, and as we share our gifts with each other—as we celebrate the gifts we are to each other—we can feel the warm bond of that embrace tighten around us. For we have heard it again and again through all those people of God who preceded us—"All things are yours, whether Paul or Apollos, or Cephas (or each other) or the world or life or death or the present or the future, all are yours; and you are Christ's; and Christ is God's."

PAUL K. PETERSON
Our Saviour's Lutheran Church
St. Paul, Minnesota

COME — SEE — HEAR — TELL
The Festival of St. Mary Magdalene
July 22
John 20:1-2, 11-18

A Messenger Is a Witness

The person who comes with a message is always a little bit special. The messenger who has himself been on the scene carries a distinct credibility. We all have known the fascination when someone has said, "And I saw it myself. I was there!"

I remember the hot August day when, from our little one-street town, we saw that great column of smoke off to the east. Soon we heard the fright-scream of the fire siren—and everyone turned to whatever neighbor was near enough to talk to. "Surely it must be a fire out in the blueberry swamp. That's about the angle—and the distance." And then came Iver Ekqvist driving in with wild eyes—and with holes burned in the fabric top of his old Model T. "I tell you, I drove right tru da fire! It vass on both sides of the road!" He was authentic. He had been there. The smell of the fire was on him!

I remember Prof. Bryan, in the university biology class: "and I reached into that cell—and with the two micro-needles, took hold of that single chromosome—and stretched it like a rubber band!" He, there, that huge man with the big voice, had himself reached into a single living cell—and moved things around at will. He had witnessed a first. He had held the probes himself!

And I can hear, as though from only moments ago, the voice of Martin Niemöller just after those terrible years in the Nazi prisons. "In every *way* we were bound. But the word of God was not bound! We had His word. And HE was there with us. Jesus was with us!" That man had known the presence of the Lord. We could hear it in his voice. He had met him. And he told us! He was a witness!

Mary Magdalene Was a Witness

We know only a few brief scenes from the life of Mary Magdalene. All of them are about one who was a witness. The reports of her are all action. Verbs! Twenty-four verbs—and all of them tell about being a witness.

She was with Jesus in his Galilean ministry. She was *with* him. She was a witness.

At some point he cast out seven demons from her. Whatever that experience was, she was there. She was the one. She was a witness.

On the day that Jesus was crucified, she stood looking on. She stood at the foot of the cross. And at the end of the day, when they were laying his body in the tomb, she was sitting opposite, and she *saw* where he was laid. She was a witness.

The next day she bought spices for anointing his body, and on the first day of the week, she went to the tomb. When she *came* to the tomb, she went over to see just how it all was. And she *saw* that the stone was rolled away. She saw what appeared to be a young man, who said, "Do not be amazed; you seek Jesus of Nazareth, who was crucified. He has risen, he is not here; see the place where they laid him. But go, tell his disciples and Peter that he is going before you to Galilee; there you will see him, as he told you." Mary Magdalene *was* a witness; and she was to *be* a witness!

And she departed with fear and joy—and ran to Peter and John, and said, "They have taken the Lord out of the tomb." She was a witness.

Then she went back to the tomb. There she stood weeping, and saw two angels in white. Then she turned around—and saw

Jesus. At first she didn't know him. But then, when he spoke her name—she *knew!* She was a witness.

And she heard him say, "Go to my brethren and say to them, I am ascending to my Father and your Father, to my God and your God." And Mary Magdalene went, and said, "I have seen the Lord." And she *told* them that he had said these things to her. She was a witness.

The Resurrection of Jesus Christ was the very central event in God's message of salvation—and Mary Magdalene was in on it! She was the first one to whom he appeared!—the prime witness of them all!

Mary Magdalene—her very name has the sound of the morning, and the fresh rosy light of a day that is new. She was there at the resurrection dawning. She was the first witness of all.

Mary Magdalene Came, Saw, Heard, and Told

Now, let's go back a moment—to think a bit what kind of person she was, she who was the first to behold our resurrected Lord. The Old Testament lesson appointed for her day in the church's remembrance, is taken from Ruth. Ruth—an outsider, of the country of Moab, not an Israelite, and one to whom was given the word, "The Lord grant that you may find a home." There was something of the homeless, something of the outsider, about Mary Magdalene too. Jesus had cast out from her seven demons. Surely there had been something about her that was homeless, searching. No wonder she had so strong a sense of *caring* about the one who had set her free from her estrangement, and lostness, and bondage.

Oh, there had been others who were freed, but most had never even come back to say thank you. And there were those who had gone about with him, but who left him, and did not come back. Even those who were closest, forsook him at the end—save only John, and his Mother, and some other women—and Mary Magdalene.

Mary Magdalene stayed by—as close as she could—at the cross, and at the tomb, and in the early resurrection morning. There she was! She had found her place to be. And she was there! She came; and she saw; and she heard—and she told! "I have seen the Lord!"

Dorothy Sayers, the great British dramatist, mystery writer, and theologian, wrote a series of radio-dramas, "The Man Born to Be King," which many regard to be the most true to scripture of all such attempts. In her notes to the players, she wrote of Mary Magdalene, "Mary Magdalene cannot *wait* to see the angels. She must run somewhere, fetch somebody, *do* something." You know someone like that—someone who must always be up and going, out and helping, off and serving—in Jesus' name. It's as though Jesus sent them himself. I guess he did. It's because they have answered, "Here am I." They have heard the Lord's word to go and tell; and they have said, "Send me."

It has wisely been observed that while everyone can say, "I am present," only a few can say, "Here am I." For to answer "Here am I," means that you no longer belong only to yourself, but that you give the presence of your being over to the One who calls you.

Mary Magdalene gave the presence of her being over to Jesus.

Mary Magdalene had heard Jesus' call.

Mary Magdalene belonged to him.

And Mary Magdalene went forth to tell his name.

Mary Magdalene was a witness. She said, "I have seen the Lord."

I Am a Witness

Now, I have to say, "How about me?"

I have been with Jesus, some. How wonderful! I haven't deserved it, for I also am a kind of outsider. But the marvel of my life is that, as it has happened, I've been brought to be with Jesus. He has reached out to me, and I have come to be near him. I am a witness.

And I have seen the Lord. I have seen his hand in the lives of many people I have known. I have seen his presence in many a moment of my own life. His forgiveness, and his freeing strength against evil, are evident to me. I am a witness.

And I have heard the call of Jesus Christ—his word, "Follow me," and his word to make disciples—baptizing them, and teaching them to pay attention to what he has commanded. His word plainly includes me. I've heard that word. I am a witness.

And I have something to tell. I am the only one who can say how Jesus has appeared to me. I am the only one who can say that *I* have seen Jesus as my Lord. I *am* the one Jesus depends on to say that. I am to be a witness.

I—am to be—a witness.

I—am to be—a witness.

C. RICHARD EVENSON
American Lutheran Church
Huron, South Dakota

YOU'RE THE GREATEST!
St. James the Elder, Apostle
July 25
Mark 10:35-45

It had been a rain-soaked spring. Heavy, wet snows and rains further north, combined with the local steady downpours, had swollen the river that flowed through the city, and the streams that fed it, to the point of overflowing.

Day by day the river rose, and as it reached flood stage the mayor of the city sounded the call for volunteers to fill sandbags and build dikes at riverfronts where businesses and homes were in danger. Workers swarmed in from all over the metropolitan area. Factories eased off on their work schedules and stores closed early to supply more manpower at the dikes.

One of the volunteers who came to the riverfront to help was a man named Martin. He recognized many of his fellow factory workers on the sandbag-brigade. It was a little like a picnic and a reunion and a night out all rolled into one. Nobody seemed to mind the exhausting pace. What little complaining was voiced was done in a spirit of good humor and jest. The spirit of camaraderie ran high.

Back to Normal

After three days at the dikes the river crested and the water began to recede. Within a week the dikes were coming down. City crews took over the job of cleaning up the sandbags. The volunteers were gone now.

Martin went back to work like the others. But the day after the crest was past he saw a film story on his local television news at 6 o'clock. What he saw startled him. In one section of the riverfront the dike had broken after the crest was past and volunteers had begun thinning out. Water had flooded a section of homes in a poor section of the city. The film story showed an old woman looking at a layer of mud on her living room floor.

After supper Martin climbed in his car and drove to the section of town he'd seen in the news report. There were street barricades when he got close to the scene and he had to get out and walk. A few minutes later he found the house he had seen on the film. The woman was struggling with her personal disaster, trying to decide whether to clean it up or give up. Martin began to talk to her. She was living alone, no family left in the world, with no place to go but this poor house. She was living on welfare and had no money to pay for cleanup of her house. Nobody had offered to help from her neighborhood.

Pitching In

Martin offered to help. The woman was delighted. She found him a shovel. As he began to carry mud out of the house, the woman took new courage to face the task and began washing the furniture and doing other small chores. Martin worked steadily until almost midnight. He wasn't nearly finished when he finally had to stop. It was a backbreaking job. He was exhausted.

"I'll be back tomorrow night," he promised the woman. "I've got to go home and get some sleep. My work day begins at 7 a.m."

Martin was good to his word. He came back the next night. And the next. By the fourth night the job was pretty well completed. After the shoveling, he brought rags and soap and helped the woman wash the walls and floor. Then he brought her some rugs and used furniture from his basement and hauled her ruined furniture to the dump.

Toward the end of the project the woman began to ask Martin some questions. "Why are you doing this for me?" she asked. "You don't even know me. You don't even *live* around here!" Martin gave some ordinary answers. "You needed help. You couldn't do it by yourself."

"But you're the only one who *came*," said the woman. Your factory has hundreds of workers like you. When the dike work was finished, none of *them* came back. Even the mayor didn't help. He drove through here one day with some of his people from city hall, inspecting the damage. But he wouldn't even get his hands dirty. He didn't even get out of his car!"

"Well," said Martin, "let me tell you the truth. I felt like I *had* to come. You see, I belong to Jesus, the Christ. He really did a lot for me, and made my life worth something. I just feel like sharing that. Right now *you're* the person I can share it with the best."

The woman shook her head. "I'm not much of a church person, understand? But if you'd do this much because of this person Jesus, all I can say is you must really think he's the greatest!"

Martin smiled and nodded. "He is." He grinned. "You bet he is!"

"And you know something else?" she interrupted, "As far as I'm concerned *you're* the greatest. Believe me, you really are."

Dirty Hands, Clean Heart

And she was right. The woman in that story had Martin pegged exactly right. He really was the greatest. Not exactly for the reason that she chose, although she was certainly entitled to her feelings of overwhelming gratitude. But Martin was the greatest for a much more profound reason. He had discovered what sorts of things make for full living, existence saturated with meaning. He understood Jesus' words: "Whoever would be great among you must be your servant." Here was a servant of Jesus who wasn't afraid to get his hands dirty, to get some blisters, to lose some sleep on behalf of another person in need. That's the stuff that greatness is made of. What's more, he dirtied his hands for the right reason: his heart was in the right place. It was in tune with the love of God, which took control of him and shaped his living. Not perfectly by any means. Martin, like all of us, is a mixture of two kinds of energy. God and the devil wrestle constantly for first place in his life. All of us are simultaneously torn in our loyalty between good and evil. The lordship of Jesus Christ guarantees the outcome in our future. But for the present we are a long way from unmixed motives when we share God's love with others.

God's person doesn't immobilize himself, however, simply because he has doubts about the purity of his motives. Suppose Martin had said, "Golly, I sure would like to help that poor woman, but she might think I was only down there to blow my own horn. And maybe I would be." The fact is, the woman needed help and Jesus wanted Martin there. Fortunately he went.

In Martin's defense, and in ours, we need to remember that regardless of our motives, Jesus makes them pure—he purifies our hearts and what comes out of them—by his own love for us. It acts like a great cleansing river that moves through us and readies us for action in the world. What God really wants from us is dirty hands and clean hearts. Those are the things that make for greatness.

Armchair or Elbow Grease?

With whom do you and I identify in the parable? If you feel as though your world is coming apart you may think you're the woman in the disaster area. But if we exclude her for a moment, it's likely that Martin is not our first choice. In fact, many of us would identify with the mayor. Interested in the woman's dilemma? Certainly. But we have a nagging feeling inside that our "interest" may be more akin to the kind of "curiosity" that brings lookers-on to fires. We're a lot like the mayor. We want to know what's going on. But we'd just as soon stay in the car, thank you. We might soil our shoes.

We're in good company. Jesus' own disciples were prone to the same sort of folly. A prime example is James, the brother of John. This is the day in the church's year on which we give James "the Elder" (since there is another James in the disciples' list also) special attention. James and John were sons of Zebedee and two of the three close inner circle members in Jesus' group. They were on hand for the transfiguration, the raising of Jairus' daughter, and the agony of Gethsemane, in each case at closer range than the other nine.

That might help to explain why James and brother John came to Jesus with what sounds to us like one of the most egotistical proposals of all time. "Teacher," they said, "we want you to do for us whatever we ask of you." If I had been Jesus at that point I would have said to myself "I can hardly wait to hear what's coming." Sure enough, it was a favor to end all favors. "Grant us to sit," they said, "one at your right hand and one at your left in your glory." The logic is understandable: Jesus had taken them into his inner circle, along with Peter (although they forgot to bring Peter along for this request, perhaps because they were a bit jealous of him and perhaps because they could only imagine there being room for two at the two sides of the Lord). If Jesus had shown them favoritism thus far, why should he not complete the gesture now? It couldn't hurt to ask.

Follow the Leader

A venerable pastor friend of mine has often cautioned "Be careful what you ask of God: he may give it to you." That would have been good advice for James. Not having noticed that Jesus was not, in his ministry, wearing crowns or mounting thrones (or perhaps supposing that would come later at Jerusalem), James literally begged Jesus to give him the same portion that Jesus himself would have. James had no idea what that would be like. Jesus did. It is interesting to speculate how James may have approached Jesus if he had had such an understanding of the future. If he had understood that he might have to die at the hands of his enemies in order to win his throne we could at least give him credit for willingness to run the gauntlet (we are not at all sure in this text that he is ready for such a choice). But even at that, Jesus' answer is the same. In effect, the reply to James is the answer given to us as well: Jesus is not in the rewards-peddling business. Greatness is not a commodity to be distributed or swapped for ready cash or in exchange for services rendered, as church power actually came to be awarded in the Middle Ages. The opposite is the case: Greatness is a result, in fact quite an incidental result, of being and doing faithfully what we are made to be and do, namely to serve and help and lift up and advocate and care about in Jesus' name. All of that, being true to ourselves, and to what makes for meaning in life, is and brings its own reward.

Jesus was a king. But he died on a cross. We don't hold a funeral service on Good Friday. When we are right-minded we have a celebration. Suffering and death for another brings its own reward. That's what greatness is made of.

James died for the faith. King Herod killed him. James is the only one of the original twelve apostles whose death for the sake of the gospel is reported in the Bible. Was that what James had had in mind when he asked Jesus to give him and his brother the same cup and the same baptism that Jesus had? We doubt it. But he ended up with exactly that. And what is stunning about it all is that, while James didn't get what he thought he was asking for, in a profound sense he really did get it—he even got the greatness he wanted. It just didn't look and feel like he imagined it would.

James told Jesus he was ready to follow the leader in exchange for greatness. He did. James learned what greatness was. It is service. And it calls to us.

MICHAEL L. SHERER
Redeemer Lutheran Church
Washburn, Iowa

FLOWERS FOR THE OSSUARY
Mary, Mother of Our Lord
August 15
Luke 1:46-55

A Little Sign of Human Hope Amid Overwhelming Sorrow

In the early seventies the newspapers reported the discovery of the bones of a crucified man, found outside of Jerusalem in a tomb opened by accident by bulldozers preparing the ground for the construction of an apartment building. The bones were found bundled together in a limestone ossuary amid many other ossuaries and the remains of many other dead. What was surprising about the discovery was that it was the first time that the bones of a crucified man have been unearthed. This is, of course, amazing because we know from historical sources that thousands of people were crucified by the Romans and others in Palestine and elsewhere in the ancient world. But here at last we were face to face with fragments of that old terror, evidence of a little bit of agony of that awful punishment. These bones—doubtless of a man named Yehochanan (John) for that name is scratched on the limestone of the ossuary exterior—these bones are dated by archeology to have come from the first century of our era, therefore from about the time of Christ.

But what was most fascinating to me about the story that appeared in the newspapers was the archeologists' report of finding in the corner of the ossuary the remains of what could probably be identified as a little bunch of flowers. These flowers were doubtless brought there and placed in the ossuary when the bones of this dead Yehochanan were, some time after his death and decay, bundled together and placed, after the burial customs of the Jews, in an ossuary. It was not only fragments of ancient oppression and terror that were found in the ossuary, then, but also little fragments of ancient hope and love. One can imagine a story behind those flowers. Perhaps a friend or a wife, a mother or a father may have brought them to that bone-bundling as a sign of mourning, but also as a sign of love and of hope and of longing—and perhaps also of prayer, prayer that this one, this Yehochanan, who by his awful death was brought to such utter degradation, brought to such absolute lowliness by some ancient and unnamed tyranny in a story that is now hidden to us, that this one might perhaps be remembered by God and lifted up, raised up from his awful sorrow.

That little story may, of course, mirror for us thousands of other stories—some known, many thousands unknown, then and now—of those who suffer and of those who suffer with those who suffer, of those who hope that suffering might know some end, that poverty might be relieved, hunger filled, injustice corrected. Those little flowers there, a sign of human hope amid an intolerable injustice, may signal for us our own hopes for the healing of harms and the righting of wrongs in our own lives and in the world that we know. But they were pathetic flowers, nonetheless. For what comes to Yehochanan's bones seems to be no comfort and no lifting up, but just the bulldozers of modern construction and the curiosity of the modern newspaper.

Mary Sings in the World of Sorrow

The bones of that ossuary, of course, were not the bones of Jesus, though he was *among* the thousands crucified and among the yet more thousands who have known injustice and sorrow in our world. Nor are the flowers in the ossuary the flowers of Mary, whom we celebrate today. But Mary was, nonetheless, one who kept watch at a cross in the time of the Romans, and among those who made her own signs of mourning and of love and hope and longing and prayer in the midst of a suffering world.

The song that is the text for us today is, of course, a song that comes from the birth of Jesus and not his death. But, lest we forget, that birth was the birth of one who came to be crucified. And the song that Mary sings, giving expression to her great joy and hope, is a song that is sung in a world filled with crucifixions and with great sorrow. The very content of her song, sung with a jubilance as if her hope were already fulfilled, bears witness to the awful circumstances which she hopes will be overcome by God himself. But is her song, then—in which she hopes for God's action in raisng up the lowly and filling the hungry and scattering the oppression of humanity—is her song only more flowers, more pathetic flowers brought to the tombs of the world? It is a song of Jewish hope, all filled with the ancient hopes of the people of God. But is it only a pathetic sign in a world where Jewish hopes are denied?

Mary Sings All the Biblical Faith

Her song is filled with all the biblical faith. Her song brings to expression the very shape of biblical faith itself: the faith that God is the one who brings creation out of nothing, life out of death, promise out of dead ends; that God is the great one of whom the whole Scripture sings; that *his* is the power to bring cosmic reversal and also to reverse even the fortunes of the littlest and lowly of the earth.

Abraham already knows that God brings life out of what seems to be the dead end of a barren life; that God's great promise is given first to one who is yet childless and then to all the descendants of that child from childlessness! Israel sings the song knowing that God chooses a little nation, a nothing, and makes it his people, bringing the people out of slavery into freedom, and opening the door for them to come into full life before him. Hannah, who had been barren, sang at the birth of Samuel that God is the one who is the God of reversals—life out of death, birth out of barrenness, something out of nothing, a people out of no people. And the exiles sang as is shown in our lesson from the Old Testament today. The exiles knew that God was the one who could bring out of exile promise and freedom and the rebuilding of Zion. And Mary herself sings for she regards herself as nothing before him—little, insignificant. And yet God chooses her, makes her his vessel, the bearer of his son.

Mary sings, then the whole of the biblical faith, brings it to expression in this simple song. All of the message of the Bible is here gathered together in her song, the song that rejoices and exalts in God who acts. She sings, then, for all of Israel—brings Israel to song—for Israel is that people which wrestles with God. And here Mary brings that wrestling to expression, that cry to God that he would indeed act, that joy in God that he has acted. Mary sings here, however, also for all hoping humanity, for all the longing earth, for all those who indeed hope for the kind of fulfillment in which she already rejoices. But where is this biblical faith? Where is the fulfillment which she speaks of as if it were already taking place? Is her song only another bouquet for the ossuaries of the world? The injustice seems to continue. The proud and the mighty are full and on their thrones yet. And the little, the hungry, those of low degree continue to be yet littler, yet hungrier, yet lower.

Her Son Is the Full Meaning of Her Song

But the full meaning of Mary's song is found most clearly, not in all those old stories—Abraham and Israel and Hannah—which she brings to expression, but in her son. For among the little ones of the earth, among the hungry ones, among the crucified ones, among those whose very life and death cries out for the justice of God in a cry seemingly yet unfulfilled, is Jesus. And the deepest meaning of the gospel we announce and celebrate here today is that God has made this little one, this crucified one, the very source of life itself. This lowly one has been exalted. This hungry one has been so filled with good things that from his fullness we may all receive. And God's mercy is so full on this one, this Jesus, that it is a mercy that pours out to all humanity. God's answer to those old and nameless hopes brought to the burial of Yehochanan is in his son. And God's fulfillment to this song of the ancient promise of the scriptures all compressed into Mary's *Magnificat* is in his son. God does not ride above the sorrow, bidding us yet believe a little longer. But he gathers the sorrow into himself, into himself as *one* of the little ones, and so begins the righting of wrongs, so begins the healing of harms. He himself shares the sorrow. He himself begins the victory in the resurrection of his son. And so he himself wipes away the tears and bids us sing the truth—not pathetic hopes but the *truth*, albeit often hidden in an unjust world, about all things.

The Church Sings with Mary: A Sign of Great Hope Amid Sorrow

On this feast today the church sings with Mary. Every evening in the ancient church when vespers were sung Mary's song was sung as well. And now especially on this feast of Mary, which we keep gladly, her song forms our central text. The flowers may be brought by the church to the ossuaries of the world. All her signs of hope, of mourning and of prayer may be sung at every place where the hungry are still empty and where the lowly are still oppressed. And the flowers of her song may be brought by us to the ossuaries of our own and our neighbors' hearts, to those anguished places where hopes go yet unfulfilled. For her song is not simply a pathetic sign of hope against hope, but her song is the truth. It is the biblical faith brought to simple and clear expression. It is the word of God which we may trust. For the word which she *sings* comes most clearly to sight and to human experience in the word which she *bears* in Jesus her son, who is God exalting those of low degree and filling the hungry with good things.

Mary is indeed blessed. And we call her so today, both because she speaks and sings the truth and because she bears that very truth of God for the world. God's mercy *is* on those who fear him. And we may pray that he may, in fact, make us the hungrier, empty us and put us down from our mighty thrones, that we might join his poor in waiting for his sure salvation, waiting together with his son.

We are invited this day to not forget Mary, this woman singing, and to not forget the revolutionary biblical vision she knows of the world: the great reversals of God.

GORDON LATHROP
Wartburg Theological Seminary
Dubuque, Iowa

WHO FOLLOWS IN HIS TRAIN?
St. Bartholomew, Apostle
August 24
John 1:43-51

This text is the reference to the conversion of Bartholomew and his call into our Lord's apostleship. In the first three Gospels, the apostle we remember on this day is called Bartholomew. In John's Gospel he is referred to as Nathanael.

Bartholomew, a Follower

In honoring Bartholomew-Nathanael, one of the Lord's twelve apostles, we honor all Christians who may think of themselves as the least important and least significant in the Lord's entourage.

If you sometimes regard yourself as hardly counting, as little more than a name on a membership list, as only a face in the congregation, then you are honored today. If you think the congregation wouldn't miss you if you didn't show up and will hardly remember you after you're gone, then you are honored today even as we honor Bartholomew.

After all, who was he? One of the forgotten of the twelve. He was not a stand-out among the twelve, not as memorable as Peter or James or John or Thomas. Who knows anything about him? I have searched the scriptures and found little.

From one point of view, he's little more than a name among the other eleven in the Gospel writer's rosters. Aside from the few brief words in our text, he spoke nothing that is quotable and did nothing that is notable. What is he beyond a face in the da Vinci portrayal of the last supper? If he had failed to show up, would you have noticed him missing?

Bartholomew represents all in the congregation who are faithful, quiet followers of Christ, but who have not and will not make the history books. If you find some kinship with him, then you should feel recognized with him today. This is so important because we honor our leaders, but fail to recognize the importance of followers.

The hymn, "The Son of God Goes Forth to War," poses the challenge, "Who follows in his train?" Of course, the question refers to Jesus' march to the cross to be sacrificed for the life of mankind. "Who follows in his train?" Who of our forebears? Who of us in our congregation?

When I was a small boy sitting in church, singing that hymn,

I wondered what was meant by Jesus' "train." You can imagine that my thoughts went to railroad tracks, to engines, cars, and cabooses. What kind of train did Jesus have, I used to wonder. Later, as I attended a few weddings and heard of the bride's train, I came to understand what "train" meant and to what the question in the hymn referred. Who of us would be among those in the Lord's following?

Possibly, like me, you think that question can be answered easily. The big names of Christianity—Peter, James, John, Paul, Martin Luther, pastors, teachers—they are the obvious followers in his train! Answers may vary a name or two, but I assume our tendency is to answer with the big names; the people who are leaders, who did great things, who wrote books and were often quoted. Who follows in his train? The leaders of the church! And that eliminates most of us.

As a pastor of some years, I can now give to the question a more accurate answer. It isn't just the leaders, the giants of the faith, who follow in his train. In fact, leaders have a special temptation which makes following Christ most difficult. They must often wrestle with enormous egos. Sometimes those self-serving egos remove them from the company following the master. Many have been destroyed because they wanted their own following. Rather than being the servants of the Lord, they become his greatest competition.

Importance of Followers

Our Lord is not asking that only a talented few take their places in his train. He is also looking to us, to common people, to people like Bartholomew.

I once took a seminary course called "Creative Teaching." It was taught, appropriately enough, by one of the most creative teachers I have ever met. He told of a weekend retreat he had conducted in a congregation. Somehow the people on the retreat ended up in their pastor's basement where he kept a well-guarded secret. He was a model train buff. Undoubtedly the pastor kept his interest in trains secret because he felt it would not fit his congregation's image of the pastoral leadership. But our leader was able to turn his hobby into a great teaching tool. As all of the retreat members became involved in the operation of the trains, he asked, "Can you relate yourself and your own discipleship to this train?" "Where are you going?" "Do you have a direction?" "Are you part of the train?" "Who is your power?"

"Who is going with you?" "Which car best describes you and what you do for the Lord in your congregation?"

A few thought they were like the engine, or at least like the coal car, trying to give power to the engine. They were the leaders. Others picked our various cars. "I'm like a passenger car," said one person, "I'm the chairman of a committee and I must move those people." Another said, "I'm a boxcar, always having to carry the freight." "We're like the maintenance car," said the trustees. But a great many people felt they didn't fit with any car, except with maybe the caboose, last in line, bringing up the rear, could be dropped off and not missed.

An important discussion followed! Those people would be missed! The caboose gives stability to the train on curves, one person suggested. Certain signals come from the caboose that are essential to the engineer, another volunteered. It's where the really important people are, they granted.

The discussion of trains soon moved on to become a discussion of congregational life. A congregation can have only one leader. There is only one who gives the direction, who sets the course, who supplies the power, and that is Christ. Everyone else in the congregation must be a follower in his train. Who can say, then, which follower is more important than another?

Who follows in his train? The stand-outs to be sure, Peter, James and John. But also those whose names and deeds, whose prayers and offerings, have hardly been remembered, like Bartholomew. And maybe like you.

We've given the impression that those who stand out are more important. It isn't so. Anyone who follows in the Lord's train is important because he is a part of the greatest movement in human history, the redemption of mankind through Christ. If you are connected to him, if you are involved in his love for the world, you are important, and you will be missed if you drop out.

Qualities of a Follower

Bartholomew, though quiet, was a loyal follower of Jesus Christ. He was steady, constant, patient, enduring. And that is certainly more important than all of the vocal, flashy disciples who followed for a while and then left him.

You don't hear much about Bartholomew. There is little more than this brief account of his conversion and call in John's Gospel. He was there as a follower, but he was there! He was there as Jesus preached the kingdom. He was there at the last meal. He was there in the upper room to greet the risen Christ.

He was there on the shore of Galilee when the risen Christ gave the directive for his train as it began to move through the centuries. Bartholomew was there, not as a leader, but as a follower.

Who follows in the Lord's train? Bartholomew! And tradition has it that this quiet, contemplative, simple, believing disciple endured a martyr's death being flayed with a knife. He may not have been a leader, not one to be readily remembered or often quoted, but he was faithful and constant, a true follower.

Dr. Alvin Rogness tells the story of a college entrance form which was to be filled out by the parents of prospective students. One father contemplated the question which read, "Would you say that your son or daughter is a leader or a follower?" The temptation for the father, of course, was to answer, "Leader." But he had to be honest. "My son is a good boy. He is constant, dependable, gets things done, but you could hardly call him a leader." So he marked, "follower." An official of the college was so impressed that he took time to write to the father, "It gives me great comfort to know that in this fall's freshman class of several hundred leaders, we can count on one follower!"

It is important for the church to sponsor leadership training for its people and to give recognition to its leaders, but in so doing we may have missed something. We've too often extolled the examples of our leaders and have neglected to honor the example of those who follow.

Bartholomew, as a follower, did not feel the need to defend his first prejudice to preserve his ego. Nothing good can come out of Nazareth, seemed his initial reaction. But that was open to change. Many of our so-called important people cannot follow Christ because they must guard their prejudice. Contemporary society has many ways to rephrase the prejudice—"If he didn't graduate from Harvard, he can't be any good." Bartholomew, in spite of his prejudice, was willing to submit to the test, "Come and see." Leadership types often assume a different attitude, "I'm a busy man, my mind's made up."

Bartholomew was a man without guile. He was honest about himself, devoid of a personal ambition that would undercut a master the minute he could be in a position to serve himself. Leaders have been known to use the congregation as a stepping stone to their own personal advancement.

Bartholomew was open to being known and to knowing the truth. Our text gives the impression that the Lord could see through him. Bartholomew didn't resist being known. Leaders, having images to protect, are often not so open.

Bartholomew was a quiet man who came to a quiet faith. Without fanfare, he came to a conviction that Jesus was the Son of God and he was not afraid to say so. Leaders are sometimes hesitant to affirm their faith publicly, depending on the popularity of Jesus at the moment.

Bartholomew was called; he continued to be called. We are impressed by well-known personalities sporting dramatic conversions. But more impressive are the conversions which continue.

Bartholomew was promised by Jesus that he would see greater things. Indeed he did. Followers have a way of seeing. It's a matter of knowing that God's great things are of a different character than the great things of men. Leaders who are accustomed to defining great things as the achievements of men may miss the simple but profound workings of God.

So on this day, we must speak in praise of all the unsung followers of Christ in our congregations. They keep the church balanced on the curves. Untainted by the aspirations of self, they set the example for all who would be followers of Christ. They are examples even for our leaders.

Who follows in his train? Not just Peter, James, and John, but also Bartholomew—and you!

LARRY A. HOFFSIS
Trinity Lutheran Church
Columbus, Ohio

CROSS YOUR HEART
Holy Cross Day
September 14
John 12:20-33

It is a matter of faith and record that Jesus gave his life on a cross for the redemption of sinful mankind. Because we are creatures who understand our existence through our senses and experiences, we naturally use "things" to help us in our awareness of what has happened to us. We make up a date for our Lord's birth, and set up a crèche to make it "real." We celebrate birthdays and light the appropriate number of candles on a cake. We take a snapshot and mark it with the date for later recalling of the event. And our ancestors in the church used both the date and the discovery of the cross to help them remember in a "sensible" way, the glory of the death of Jesus Christ.

In today's Gospel Jesus' words are recorded: "And I, when I am lifted up from the earth will draw all men to myself." That brought all people into the *purpose* of that exaltation of the cross. The use of the sign of the cross at Baptism, at invocations and benedictions, repeats over and over again what this once-a-year observance of Holy Cross Day proclaims. The hymns we still use, out of many that set the cross as theme, illustrate how it is the sign of redemption, not the means of crucifixion that is central—"In the cross of Christ I glory" or "The royal banners forward go" for example.

The Second Lesson in 1 Corinthians 1:18-24 reminds us that it is folly not to consider the cross if we wish to avoid perishing. Isaiah 45:21-25 reminds us that "every knee should bow" to the God who has highly exalted him who was crucified. The Gospel, John 12:20-33 gives us occasion from our Lord's dying awareness to consider how we who have "crossed our hearts" should "hope to die."

Cross Your Hearts and Hope to Die

Only reluctantly do we actually accept what it means to "see Jesus." When the Greeks came to see Jesus, Philip heard their requests, hesitated, and took them to Andrew, and together they brought them before him. The Lord is not quoted by the evangelist as engaging in any "hello" or chit-chat about their homeland. He moves at once to assert that "seeing is believing." "If you want to see me, then cross your heart and hope to die." No one really sees Jesus unless he realizes that he had taken on life in order to die, and called followers to join him in bearing the cross.

If You Really Want to See Jesus, You Must See the Cross

Jesus said, "The hour has come for the Son of man to be glorified. Truly, truly, I say to you, unless a grain of wheat falls into the earth and dies, it remains alone; but if it dies, it bears much fruit." We understand Jesus—he is giving a summary of the purpose of his life and death.

A seminarian in a sermon on Holy Cross day described our all-too-common reaction. He used our terms, but the tempter's logic. "Get on the stick, Jesus." "Be the world leader you've got it in you to be. Show them all. Cut out that stuff about suffering. Get on the stick."

And what was Jesus' response? He pointed out that death was all around—"Now is the judgment of this world." And he made it clear that he had come to bring life—"Now shall the ruler of this world be cast out; and I, when I am lifted up from the earth, will draw all men to myself." Add it up, and what he said was, "Get thee behind me, Satan, with all that talk about my avoiding my holy cross day." And, having said that, he got on the stick, all right, climbed up on that stick, that cross!

If you would see Jesus you must see the cross. That even applied to God, his Father, once he was committed to the cross as the means of redemption. How must it have looked to God, transcendant God, in his awe-ful majesty, God who fills all things, looking as we must say, "down"? There, a little east of the Mediterranean, a mound in Palestine, a stick stuck into Golgotha. "This is My Beloved Son. Crucify Him." And his Son, Jesus, transfixed. He, the Son of God, right enough, got on the stick—yes, without sin, save ours, save the world's, to save the world, to save us.

But the Gospel does not let us go.

If You Would Follow Jesus, You Must Take Up the Cross

"Of course, you Greeks; you, Philip, Andrew; all of you, if you're just *looking*. . . . But if you would follow me, you must take up my cross."

Imagine seed protesting being sown. You stand there in your well-raked lawn, the seed in your hand. And suddenly you hear the seed refusing to be cast into the little furrows, refusing to be covered by earth and sodden by water, to die. What would you say? "Why do you think I bought you? What did you think I had in mind?" What would God say? "What do you think I made you for?"

Seed: "I'd rather be in a botany classroom, you know—in a glass bottle with a big cork stopper, along with other bottles for all to see. I'd like to be special, labeled, unique. We all would, all of us seed, seed of Adam, seed of Abraham, seed of Luther. Winter wheat, spring wheat, strange varieties, all labeled with Latin names. Labeled Lutheran wheat, Saxon wheat, odd hybrids like Black Lutheran, Cuban Lutheran, Chinese Lutheran, even Norwegian Lutheran. Inner city Lutheran, rural weedless wheat. The Missouri strain—different bottles for the different factions, all different, but all knowing page 15 and all announcing for communion. SBH wheat, second setting; and the mutants of ILCW. That's what we all want, each our own glass bottle with a big cork stopper. We love our lives and don't want to lose them."

Jesus: "No! If you would follow me, you must be buried,

drowned and die. Except you do . . . unless that happens . . . you remain alone. Why do you think I bought you? What do you think I made you for?"

And if we, seeds all of us, should say to Jesus, "It is all very well for you to talk. You knew that you would be raised by the glory of the Father." If we would complain about dying and say, "This is a hard saying—'He who loves his life loses it, and he who hates his life in this world will keep it for eternal life.' This wasn't your real life, here on earth—you came from the Father and were going to him." If we would be very blunt with Jesus and say, "It's easy for you to say that, because for you—just three days and you would rise again." If we said all that, what would our Lord say to us?

"What do you think I have in mind for you?"

GEORGE W. HOYER
Concordia Seminary in Exile
St. Louis, Missouri

TRANSFORMED BY LOVE
St. Matthew, Apostle and Evangelist
September 21
Matthew 9:9-13

How strange it is that out of all of humanity Jesus chose twelve simple, unimpressive men to be the bearers of the great Good News to mankind. How odd that he shunned the educated and the eloquent to call to his side rough fishermen, young hotheads, and even a crooked tax collector. A more unlikely assortment of men could not be imagined. And to them he committed the keys of the kingdom!

One Who Could Write

So simple were they that there is no evidence in the scriptures that any of them could even read or write: none, that is, except for the tax collector Levi, who became the disciple Matthew. It was Matthew who remembered the words of Jesus and wrote them down so they would not be lost. Perhaps he even took notes as Jesus spoke. We would expect a tax collector to keep good records!

From the earliest days of the church it was always believed that the disciple Matthew was indeed the author of the first of the New Testament Gospels which bears his name. If that is so, what a priceless gift he gave to mankind! Of all the Gospels, that of Matthew gives us the most complete record of the life and words of Jesus. Perhaps this is why it has been placed first among the books of the New Testament. Numerous sayings of Jesus, the Sermon on the Mount and The Great Commission are recorded only in the Gospel of Matthew. Today we remember that disciple, the one who could write, and we rejoice in the gift of the great Gospel that he has given us.

Matthew the Unlikely

Of all the twelve disciples, Matthew would surely have been voted least likely to succeed in the business of holiness. He was known all around Capernaum as a crook, a grafter and a cheat. If Jesus had chosen his disciples by the standards an employer would use today in hiring an employee, he would *never* have picked Matthew!

Matthew was a tax collector and in Galilee in Jesus' time that was the most odious of all professions: about on the same level with prostitution and armed robbery. Tax collectors were the henchmen of the Roman conquerors, hired by the Romans to extort money from an impoverished people. Maybe Matthew was an agent of the hated puppet-king, Herod Antipas, who bled the people to pay off the Romans.

Tax collectors were the Mafia of their time. They were given free rein to overcharge the people and keep a generous amount for their own pockets. Graft and extortion were their stock-in-trade.

No wonder the Jewish people hated tax collectors! They were traitors to their nation. They served the oppressor and amassed great fortunes by robbing the people. So they were forbidden to enter a synagogue. They could not make an offering in the Temple. Their testimony was not accepted in Jewish courts. They were outcasts: pariahs among their own people. Today the Internal Revenue Service is hardly the most popular agency of our federal government, but our tax collectors are not held in abject hatred as were Matthew and his professional colleagues in Jesus' time.

Two Little Words

Tax collecting then was a dirty business, but imagine how hard it must have been to be a tax collector: to be hated, despised and shunned by almost everyone—to be cut off even from religion. It must have been an empty, desolate life.

One day Jesus was traveling through Capernaum, on the main road from Damascus to Caesarea. There at the city gate was the toll-booth. All goods coming into the city—salt, fish, grain—were examined and a portion was taken from each load according to the whim of the tax collector.

That day, sitting in the toll-booth, was a man named Levi, also called Matthew ("gift of God"). Jesus stopped and said to him, "Follow me." "And he rose and followed him"—to the end of his life.

That was the briefest invitation a person ever received. Just two little words: "Follow me." Yet it was enough.

Matthew the traitor, Matthew the crook, Matthew the hated was called by Jesus. In this most unlikely of men Jesus saw a child of God and a messenger for the kingdom. Matthew was a failure, but Jesus meant him for something better. He did not condone his way of life, but neither did he reject him because of it. Instead, Jesus *accepted* Matthew and trusted him to become one of his closest disciples. Only two little words were necessary: "Follow me!"

Amazed by Grace

Never before had Matthew seen such amazing grace! He recognized love when he saw it, and he followed Jesus. Here was One to whom he could give his life and soul. Everyone else rejected him, but Jesus said "Follow me." Wherever Jesus walked among men he sought out the pathetic people who had been relegated to the garbage-heap of society: prostitutes, tax collectors, lepers, the poor, the sick and the dying. Jesus knew what it was to be "despised and rejected of men."

So Matthew left a secure life and a lucrative job to set out on a hazardous and uncertain journey. He had no idea what the future might hold in store for him, but he put his life in the hands of God. Matthew was blessed that day in Capernaum when Jesus called him to his side, and all mankind has been blessed through Matthew and through his Gospel.

Love Reaches Out

Later that night Jesus sat down at dinner. (Luke says that it was at Matthew's house.) "Many tax collectors and sinners came and sat down with Jesus and his disciples." Nothing could have been more scandalous! No decent Jew would have even set foot inside the house of a tax collector, but Jesus welcomed the *un*-welcomed to his table.

Word of what was happening at Matthew's house quickly got around town. Soon some Pharisees came to see this spectacle with their own eyes. "Why does your teacher eat with tax collectors and sinners?" they asked the disciples. When Jesus saw them and heard their question, he said, "Those who are well have no need of a physician, but those who are sick. . . . For I came not to call the righteous, but sinners."

This was dangerous and revolutionary talk to the Pharisees. According to their religion a sinner was to be condemned and cast out of the ranks of the righteous, and a tax collector was the lowest kind of sinner. But Jesus *received* sinners and ate with them. Why?

It was because *love* demanded it! Isolating this tax collector, condemning him and ostracizing him would never redeem him from the sordid life he was living. Someone must reach out to him, in *love*. Someone must say to him, "You are accepted!"

The pride and lovelessness of those who condemned Matthew was certainly a greater affront to God, a greater transgression, than the thievery of this tax collector. There is a lesson here, and a warning, for those of us who regard ourselves as "religious" people. God's amazing grace transcends the pride and lovelessness of men, even of "religious" men.

Struck by Grace

Scripture tells us very little about Matthew, and nothing at all about his life before Jesus called him to discipleship. But it could well be, if truth were known, that he was a restless, empty man: the kind of man who was transformed by the grace, the love of God.

Paul Tillich once spoke of this grace in a sermon entitled "You Are Accepted" *(The Shaking of the Foundations,* p. 153ff). "Grace strikes us when we are in great pain and restlessness," he said. "It strikes us when we walk through the dark valley of a meaningless and empty life. It strikes us when we feel that our separation is deeper than usual, because we have violated another life. . . . It strikes us when our disgust for our own being, our indifference, our weakness, our hostility, and our lack of direction . . . have become intolerable to us. It strikes us when, year after year, the longed-for perfection of life does not appear, when the old compulsions reign within us as they have for decades, when despair destroys all joy and courage. Sometimes at that moment a wave of light breaks into our darkness, and it is as though a voice were saying: 'You are accepted. *You are accepted.*' . . . If that happens to us, we experience *grace.*"

This was the light that came to Matthew: the light of grace. This was the voice—the voice of grace—which spoke just two words: "Follow me." Matthew recognized love when he saw it and he followed. That love transformed him! Today we call him *Saint* Matthew—*Holy* Matthew.

CHARLES R. ANDERS
All Saints Lutheran Church
Tamarac, Florida

OUR GUARDIAN ANGELS
St. Michael and All Angels
September 29
Revelation 12:7-12

For the preacher:

Note 1: Because the apocalyptic language of the book of Revelation is "unfamiliar territory" to most Lutherans, *and* because most Lutherans do not attend adult Bible Class, *and* because so much weird theology claiming to be grounded in the book of Revelation continues to proliferate in print, *and* because the scientific spirit of our century makes it difficult for today's Christians to take seriously the "unseen element" in God's creation, *and* because the six verses of today's Second Lesson can be grasped best if they are set within the context of the six verses that precede them in chapter 12, *and* because Revelation 12:1-12 is a glorious summary of salvation history, *and* because there is ample historical precedent for an expository approach to preaching, THEREFORE I have built into much of the following sermon a straightforward, verse-by-verse explanation of the text. But the sermon will achieve its purpose *only* if the preacher sees to it that every one of his hearers has in hand a mimeographed copy of Revelation 12:1-12, *with each verse numbered.* If these verses are not before them, hearers will soon get lost in the maze of the material he is trying to illuminate.

Note 2: The four Bach cantatas referred to in the sermon's introduction are Numbers 19, 50, 130, and 149. All are available on LP records (complete with English and German texts) from the

Musical Heritage Society; MHS Building; Oakhurst, New Jersey 07755. These cantatas provide magnificent inspirational background material for the preacher as he approaches, and prepares his sermon for, the Feast of St. Michael.

Note 3: The securing in advance of slides of artists' renditions of the "victorious Michael," whether from Coventry and Ulm Cathedrals or elsewhere, will be well worth the effort.

Among the 179 cantatas Johann Sebastian Bach composed for the Sundays and feast days of the Christian Year, four were prepared for today's Feast of St. Michael and All Angels. All four focus on today's Second Lesson, from the book of Revelation, in which we read of that great war in heaven, with Michael and all his angels fighting against the dragon. The music for all four cantatas is intense, reflecting the fierceness of war; but it is also triumphant, reflecting the biblical claim that God's angels have defeated their adversary, the devil.

These cantatas were all written nearly 250 years ago, in the early 18th century. Since then, the scientific spirit of our time has become so prominent that we, unlike Bach, find it difficult to take seriously the many scriptural references to principalities and powers, and to the battles between the invisible forces of good and evil, battles which the Bible says have a direct effect on our individual and national life.

The language of the book of Revelation is largely apocalyptic. That means that it takes the power of evil very seriously, and it does not place much confidence in our human ability to overcome it. God alone, through his direct and indirect action in history, can enable good to win out over evil. And he *has* acted, through the death and the resurrection of his Son. And he *will* act, fully and finally and forever on the day of his Son's return to earth to judge both the living and the dead. The book of Revelation does not portray Jesus as the suffering servant, but as the exalted and ruling Lord, who is in control of history whether it appears that way to us or not.

My guess is that few of you have ever read the entire book of Revelation. And if you are among the few who have done so, you probably scratched your head in bewilderment, wondering what it was all about. We cannot study the entire book within the short time of a sermon; but each of you has a copy of chapter 12, verses 1 to 12, so that we might "walk" through these verses together to get the whole picture of what is going on here. If you are ever going to appreciate Michael and all his angels as a vital part of God's plan for our salvation, you've got to appreciate the difficulty of what we're up against in our lives as Christians. It's not just a daily struggle between the old and the new Adam in each of us. It is a struggle between the Holy One and the evil one, between all the powers of heaven and all the powers of hell. And the small part of this struggle that you and I can see with our eyes is only the tip of the iceberg. Come along with me, then, as we ponder these twelve verses together.

Verse 1. John, the author of Revelation, sees in a vision the one over whom the great battle between the Holy One and the evil one is being fought. She is "a woman clothed with the sun." This is a symbolic expression for all the people of God, at first only Jewish, but now including both Jews and gentiles.

Verse 2. From among the people of God there comes a child, the child you and I know from the Gospels as Jesus the Christ.

Verse 3. A great red dragon appears on the scene when this child is still an infant. The dragon's seven heads and seven diadems symbolize his craftiness and his dreadful might. He has both brain power and brute power.

Verse 4. Already as an infant this child is being tracked by the red dragon, which brings to mind that terrible story of King Herod's slaughter of all the infants in Bethlehem, in his desperate attempt to kill the child Jesus.

Verse 5. Herod's mass murder of infants fails to accomplish its purpose, but the red dragon persists. Immediately following Jesus' baptism the devil tries no less than three times to divert him from his mission as the Messiah. He tries again in the garden of Gethsemane, the night before Jesus' death. But his efforts come to nothing. The crucified Jesus is raised by God from the dead and received in triumph again in heaven. "Caught up to God and to his throne," is the way John puts it. And now this child rules at the right hand of the Father, as we say in the Creed. He rules all nations, whether they know it or not, whether they acknowledge him or not.

Verse 6. "The woman fled into the wilderness." Again, this is symbolic language for a truth most of us have experienced at one time or another when we have tried to be faithful followers of Christ. That truth is that it can be very lonely if we insist on resisting the devil, the world, and our sinful flesh. To be in the world but not of the world is a tough assignment. But there will come a time when our temptation will end. The 1,260 days symbolizes God's promise that on the day of his choosing the victory that he has already won through the blood of the Lamb will be contested no more, by no one, visible or invisible.

Verse 7. You would suppose that by this time the red dragon would have quit in disgust. Yet here he is, still tracking the Holy One of God, the child, right on up into heaven following Jesus' ascension. This time, however, Michael and all his angels enter the fray against the dragon and all his angels. What a fierce struggle that must have been! But never mind. It's over now.

Verses 8 and 9. The devil and his angels are literally thrown out of heaven in defeat. Now you can see why this section of chapter 12 has been designated by the church to be the Lesson for this day. It focuses on the reassuring truth that even though the devil has countless unseen helpers to do his dirty work for him in the world, God also has his countless unseen helpers to assist us in beating down Satan under our feet. And chief among these helpers from heaven is the angel Michael.

Verses 10 and 11. There is a great victory cheer among the martyrs. "Now the salvation and the power and the authority of Christ have come, for the accuser of our brethren has been thrown down. And they have conquered him by the blood of the Lamb." The brethren here are the martyrs who refused to turn against their Lord in time of persecution and who consequently lost their lives. Although it seemed as though they were losers, according to the vision of John here it is they who now have the last laugh, a laugh that will last to all eternity.

Verse 12. The gates of heaven are now closed forever to the dragon. The war in heaven is over. So those who dwell there can rejoice. But with us here on earth the mopup operation continues. Satan has lost the war; but he keeps right on trying to do among us as much damage as he can, because his days are numbered. His time is short, and he is filled with wrath!

That concludes our quickie course of Bible Study. I've guided you through these twelve verses because they're a dramatic summary of salvation history. They tell us what has been going on in heaven and on earth since the time of creation. They tell us how we fit into the picture. But, most important, they tell us what the future holds in store for us who now share in the victory of the Lamb who was slain, whose blood has made us free to be people of God.

Today, September 29th, we express our special gratitude to God for the help his holy angels give us day by day, the help that we ask for every time we pray in Luther's Morning and Evening Prayers, "Let thy holy angel be with me, that the wicked foe may have no power over me." I am reminded of the cartoon I saw recently that shows a burglar about to enter the living quarters of an Anglican priest. As the burglar stealthily opens the front door, the first thing his flashlight shines on is a large sign on the wall, a sign that says: "Beware! Guardian angels on duty all night!" And so they are—not only all night, but all day too. We have God's own word for it (Psalm 91:11) that he gives his angels charge over us to guard us in all our ways.

Artists through the centuries have been inspired by this dramatic image of the angel Michael, standing in triumph with sword in hand, his one foot resting on the defeated body of the dragon he has slain. I have set up our slide projector here so that I can show you two powerful contemporary sculptures of "the victorious Michael." Each speaks for itself.

The first of these sculptures *(show slide)* is the exterior wall at the entrance to the cathedral in Coventry, England. *(Pause for people to contemplate.)* And the second *(change to second slide)* hangs high above the nave on the inside rear wall of the cathedral in Ulm, Germany. I've never visited the Coventry cathedral, but my wife and I did get to Ulm several years ago during our "Organ Lofts tour of Europe." I remember how greatly impressed we both were by this *(point to Ulm slide, which is still on screen)* gigantic visual aid. It almost seemed to be shouting down to us as we were leaving the building: "Now remember this! As you go back out into the world again, you are not alone. Nor are you helpless. God is with you. His Son who died for you lives and rules. His Spirit, given to you by your baptism, lives in your heart. And lest you forget, I, Michael, Chief of Staff for the heavenly hosts of angels, have decisively defeated the evil one who keeps trying to get you to be unfaithful to your Lord. Take heart! The future belongs to God, and to you, his children."

Taking heart is one thing, and that's good! But becoming overconfident is another thing, and that's bad! Even though the devil's time here on earth is short, he has not stopped prowling around like a roaring lion (2 Peter 5:8-9), "seeking someone to devour." And, as today's text warns, he is filled with wrath. He is still capable of doing great damage.

The situation is similar to that on a deep sea fishing boat, when a huge fish has been hooked and finally hauled on board after the grueling struggle to reel it in has ended. The elated fisherman knows that the fish is his. But until it has breathed its last, he also knows that it is still capable of some wild, dangerous flapping about. He is confident, but he is also careful!

So you and I are confident as the people of God. Thanks to the Lamb whose blood was given for us, thanks to the victory of Michael and his angels in the heavenly war that followed, we can sing right along with the martyrs of old: "The salvation and the power and the kingdom of our God and the authority of his Christ have come; for the accuser, our adversary, Satan, has been thrown down!" But we are also well-advised to keep on praying along with our singing, asking our heavenly Father to "let his holy angel be with us, that the wicked foe may have no power over us."

LOUIS NUECHTERLEIN
Cheshire Lutheran Church
Cheshire, Connecticut

CARING FOR THE MIDDLESCENT
St. Luke the Evangelist
October 18
Luke 1:1-4; 24:44-53

Scene: A doctor's office

RECEPTIONIST: Mr. Ted Philips? Dr. Lucas will see you now.

TED PHILIPS: Thank you. I've been waiting . . .

DR. LUCAS: Hello Ted, how are you today?

TED: Well, Doc, I'll tell you. I'm really feeling down. Been that way for a long time. I need some help.

DR. LUCAS: What seems to be the problem?

TED: Seems like everything—my job, marriage, health—it's all going downhill.

DR. LUCAS: Tell me about it.

TED: I'm not going anywhere in my job. Been there 25 years. I made it to Vice President in Charge of Sales—but that's been the ceiling. And I feel betrayed. The company made a lot of promises and got my hopes up—but now younger guys are passing me by. I'll be lucky if they don't drop me.

DR. LUCAS: Please go on.

TED: My wife Ethel and I hardly know each other. I spent all those years trying to make it to the top and she was busy with the kids.

All we ever do is watch TV together.

And my health—this pain in my shoulder aches all the time. Maybe you saw in the paper that my neighbor Bill Eckler dropped dead last week at 43. I'm already 45—my picture will probably be in that obituary column soon.

I just don't know Doc. It doesn't seem fair. I've been looking forward to this time in my life so long, and now that it's here—what a disappointment. It's all downhill.

DR. LUCAS: Ted, I can understand why you're feeling so low, but let's face this difficulty together, try to make some sense out of it, and find some reason for joy instead of despair.

The Middle Age Crisis

This imaginary conversation between Dr. Lucas and Ted Philips exposes a very real condition for those persons who find themselves in a stage of life known as middlescence. Occurring somewhere around 40, this crisis of the middle years brings with it gnawing questions: "Is this all there is to life?" "Have I failed to make it?" "Does life really begin at 40 or is it just the beginning of the end?" Middlescence can be a time of disappointed hopes and frustration over the failure to find expected fulfillment and security. Producing this trauma is the person's growing awareness of death. From the mid-life perspective, both horizons of life are plainly visible, and the middle-ager begins to mark his days from the setting of the sun rather than its rising. Thus comes the "downhill slide."

What About St. Luke the Evangelist?

But how does this conversation between Dr. Lucas and Ted Philips and this talk of middlescence relate to this day in the Church Year given for the honor of St. Luke the Evangelist? The link is found in the tradition that St. Luke is also Doctor Luke, a gentile physician and faithful companion of Paul the Apostle.

In the introduction to his Gospel Luke presents the purpose of his work as explained to Theophilus:

> Inasmuch as many have undertaken to compile a narrative of the things which have been accomplished among us, just as they were delivered to us by those who from the beginning were eyewitnesses and ministers of the word, it seemed good to me also, having followed all things closely for some time past, to write an orderly account for you, most excellent Theophilus, that you may know the truth concerning the things of which you have been informed (Luke 1:1-4).

Ostensibly Luke writes for a patron named Theophilus, who may have been a Roman official. However, since the name means "Beloved by God," Theophilus may also be considered a representative for the Christian community to which Luke addresses his Gospel. For those readers confused about Jesus, the Doctor intends to provide order, and for those bewildered about what is happening to the church he offers knowledge of the truth.

The Church as Middlescent Patient

The implication of the introduction is that Dr. Luke is offering treatment for a church body suffering from the difficulties of the middle-age crisis similar to those of Ted Philips and other middlescents. The Gospel according to Luke was written in the early 80s of the first century, some 50 years after the death and resurrection of Jesus Christ. Jesus had risen, but where was he? Why had not death and evil been defeated and the glorious reign of the heavenly King begun? The 50 years since Christ's death and resurrection had been filled with persecutions and continued stuggles for his followers. Their hopes were disappointed, their dreams unfulfilled. It looked as though God's promised redemption of his people had fallen short. No victorious climax had come. "What's the use?" "Why go on?" "It's all downhill from here." These were the cries Dr. Luke heard from his middlescent church.

Middlescents Still

Luke's first century church is not the only one suffering from the middlescence syndrome. A similar diagnosis for our church today is often just as valid. For who in the church today doesn't know the pain of disappointed hopes? What happened to those great dreams we had? Like those "first units" which 15 years later we realized would be the hard-to-pay-off "last units." Or that "marvelous educational program" which in a few short years would revive our lay leadership and produce a flock eager for Bible study and service—instead its impact consisted of a few leftover notebooks and a few memories of what "might have been if only . . ." How about that excited new board member who attends his first church council meeting to discover that most of the time is spent in search of answers to two persistent questions: "Where will we get the money?" and "Who is willing or has the time to do it?" Or the young couple who hopes to find some meaningful relationships in the church, only to discover that the others are more messed up than they. We are still middlescent and still have lots of disillusionment and disappointment. The cries in Luke's church echo in ours: "Who cares?" "Why bother?" "Keep the roof from leaking, the pulpit filled, and the oil bill paid—that's about all there is. I'll stay home and watch TV, thank you."

There are successes in the church too, but always the ache of what might have been. The years pass and with them go a lot of the expectations. Don't hope for much, and you won't be disappointed. And here we are—in middlescence.

Dr. Luke's Prognosis: We Grow Like a Lobster

Dr. Luke had better get to work. There are a lot of middleagers in trouble: Ted Philips, Theophilus, and the church then and now. Have we any hope for renewal? New life? Real purpose? Meaning? Joy, even? Back to the original conversation between Dr. Lucas and Ted Philips. If the Doc had his practice along the rocky seacoast of Maine, he might use the following analogy in offering treatment for Ted:

DR. LUCAS: Ted, do you know that we grow like a lobster?

TED: What?

DR. LUCAS: Yes, a lobster grows by developing and shedding a series of hard, protective shells. Each time it expands from within, the confining shell must be sloughed off. And during that period of time in which the new shell develops, the lobster is left exposed and vulnerable. But he has to take that risk on his way to new security. Ted, the crisis that you are now facing—that of middle age—is not only predictable, it is desirable. Right now you face the decision of staying in the old shell and the safety that comes in staying—though with the safety there will also be frustration and stagnation

—or you can take the risk of growing and endure the pain that comes with such a transition.

TED: Where will that lead me?

DR. LUCAS: To the discovery of the truth that the only real security is an inner security rather than the externals of job or money. It will lead to the discovery of purpose and meaning found in caring for needs of others rather than absorption with your own.

The Church Grows Like a Lobster

As the lobster grows, so grows the church of God. According to Dr. Luke, God's plan of salvation for his people progresses through a series of difficult growth stages. Each stage takes the church closer to the final fulfillment of God's kingdom and the ultimate security.

In the second half of today's gospel reading, Luke conveys his prognosis for the middlescent church in the words of Jesus to his disciples in a post-resurrection appearance. He suggests the first stage of growth includes the activity of God in the life of his people for centuries past—through the Exodus, monarchy, exile—times of tension and difficulty which aided the movement of God's people toward the fulfillment of salvation.

> Then Jesus said to them, "These are my words which I spoke to you, while I was still with you, that everything written about me in the law of Moses and the prophets and the psalms must be fulfilled" (Luke 24:44).

He continues and describes the next stage:

> Then he opened their minds to understand the scriptures, and said to them, "Thus it is written, that the Christ should suffer and on the third day rise from the dead, and that repentance and forgiveness of sins should be preached in his name to all nations, beginning from Jerusalem. You are witness of these things. And behold, I send the promise of my Father upon you; but stay in the city, until you are clothed with power from on high" (Luke 24:45-49).

This new stage of growth was begun with the life and ministry of Jesus Christ. With his death and resurrection, God ushers in a new age for his people—an age characterized by the active presence of God and the joyful response of his people. The new age has begun, but it is not fully completed. It steadily moves on to its fulfillment as the ministry of Jesus Christ continues in the ministry of the church which "preaches repentance and forgiveness of sins to all nations." The church is in that transition between the sloughing off of the old shell and the completion of the new one, which means it is a time of vulnerability and pain. The new shell will not be complete until Christ returns at the end of the end-time to bring to fulfillment this new age. Until that time the church continues its Christ-like mission. Luke describes the expansion of that mission activity in his second volume entitled *The Acts of the Apostles*.

Not Alone in the Mission

As we are actively involved in continuing the ministry of Christ, we move with some difficulty and pain toward the fulfillment of the new age. But Dr. Luke assures us that we will make it through the crisis of this stage. Why? Because Jesus made it. Jesus as portrayed in Luke's Gospel is the Son with whom the Father maintained continual contact. Even through his suffering and death, Jesus was never alone, never forsaken by his loving Father. And the resurrection and ascension of Jesus is the sign of God's sure victory and of the certainty of God's promises to all his sons and daughters. As we look ahead to death, we can be sure that the Father who has shown his power and love to Jesus Christ will come through also for us. We, the people of the middlescent church can look to the sunset of our lives and be confident that with the setting of the sun also comes a new rising.

But Now Be Prepared

A contemporary greeting card for middle-agers on the outside cover features an elderly Boy Scout with camping equipment draped all over his sagging body. His spindly legs hang out of his khaki shorts and his spongy stomach over his belt. He looks worn and bewildered. Beneath him are the words: "At your age . . ." and inside it reads, ". . . what is there to be prepared for?"

"What is there to be prepared for?" asks the middlescent church. Dr. Luke's response is as bold and exciting as that of Jesus. "I send the promise of my Father upon you . . . you are clothed with power from on high."

This is the most important promise for us to hang on to; this is the promise that will not be disappointed—the promise of God's continuing presence. The Spirit of our risen Lord goes with us as Jesus Christ continues his ministry through us to all the world, all societies, and all people. Therefore, Luke's most encouraging word to us is this one: "Middle-aged church, you are the one God calls for his purpose of redeeming the world. He will bring you through, but be prepared. Prepared for difficulty and pain and prepared for a vigor, freshness, and joy which only God can provide. Be prepared, for the lobster is growing—the new shell of security and peace is being well formed. The second half of life is the best and getting better."

For that good word to Ted, Theophilus, and to us, thank you, Dr. Luke!

LOWELL J. TIMM
Grace Lutheran Church
Auburn, Maine

PEACE IS AN AGGRESSIVE WORD!
St. Simon and St. Jude, Apostles
October 28
John 14:21-27

A Measure of Peace

Once there was a man who had all the good breaks one could ask for in life. He had wealth, health and ample opportunity to pursue happiness. He found many wants in his life, but he found occasion to satisfy every one of them. He knew anxiety in his wanting, but fulfillment in his receiving. He lived long and happily and healthily until one night he died painlessly of a heart attack.

Another man lived within the identical life span of the first. He never knew privilege, was born with a handicap, had difficulty with health and wealth through all his days. He had little opportunity to fulfill his personal wants and yet managed in spite of his handicap to bring brightness and joy into the lives of many others by virtue of his happy disposition and the vocation he found in spite of his deformity.

Which of the two would you say was "happiest"?

Which of the two would you speak of as "most at peace"?

I do not ask which if either (or both) went to heaven. I ask no opinion about everlasting life. I am interested now only in asking about which may have been the "peace-full" one.

The idea of God has deliberately *not* been introduced into these lives to keep the question clean for the moment of any insinuation of godliness or ungodliness. What would you say of them?

Peace Defined in Negatives

We have been conditioned to feel that we *ought* to speak of the second one as being the happiest or most peaceful or best off.

In our heart of hearts, though, we know which life we would choose if we had a choice. With good reason our choices turn in the direction of the first and we shun the condition of the second life. Without denying that the second man *could* be as "happy" and as "peaceful" as the first, we seek after and hope for a life like the first. The second life is a "destiny" some must live with, but hardly a "choice" most of us would make.

The reason is that we define life as we would like it more by negatives than by affirmations. "Peace" is defined largely as lack of illness, absence of suffering whether physical or emotional, avoidance of indebtedness, etc. Even our positive attempts at defining life plays off these negatives: having enough money to get what we want and avoid debt, having health so we can move freely and painlessly, having people around to care for us and love us. The positives are merely the opposite sides of the negatives.

Peace Defined in Affirmatives

Because that is so, we overlook an important part of the way I have described the second person's life. The first person's life was largely described in terms of the negatives just mentioned, and that is what made it attractive. The second person's life was at least in part defined as taking its meaning from relationships with others. He brought joy and pleasure and affirmation to make the lives of other people better.

The second, then, did not particularly "conquer" anything or live well by standards we set up. He died with his handicap, never having received the "fulfillments" of the first.

Yet he knew "fulfillments" of another sort. They were in behalf of others at his own expense. He turned his handicap into a service for others and brightened the lives of others through his disposition. He expanded the lives of others in ways they did not expect by using what was given to him, little though that seemed to be. It was enough.

Peace as a "Gift"

We see something important about peace in both lives. One does not find peace inside him/herself. It is a "given" that comes to a person. The first man's "peace," as we have defined it in terms of the negatives, was his by virtue of the "gifts" that were given to him aside from what he found within himself. His happiness and peace was a "given" of health, wealth, etc.

The second man also found his "peace" outside himself . . . not so much in this case by what was "given" to him in the crippled condition or the poverty, but rather by what he was able to "give away." It was not a condition within him so much as it was an opportunity he laid hold of outside himself that enabled the "peace" to be present. The more others found in him something to make their lives whole, the more he found within himself the fulfillment of life that led to his peace. It was not a treasure discovered within so much as an opportunity he found outside his own troubled being.

That is an important element of peace . . . it is passed from one to another more than dug up from within oneself. A parent passes on to a child a sense of peace or a restlessness that the child rather quickly picks up. It is more than a word . . . it is a sense of being, a sense of acceptance, a sense of wholeness, a sense of harmony with everything around. Peace comes within the framework of relationships and is a sense of totality of being, a sense of well-being that is derived from being accepted and encouraged and received by the environment within which one lives. It is more than an absence of negatives, but above all it is a presence of positive forces that brings us to a sense of peace.

Peace as a Gift of God

We intentionally avoided introducing God into the lives of those two we spoke of earlier. Since they are, of course, made-up lives, I will now put God into both their lives and ask what it means to introduce such a dimension into their—or your and my—lives.

We read in the text that peace is spoken of by Jesus specifically as a "gift" to be received. "My peace I give to you; not as the world gives do I give to you." Whether it comes from the world or from him, peace is a gift, Jesus says. Here he affirms the positive definition of peace in a way that forces the question of where such peace originates.

The Bible describes "peace" as the state of affairs that prevails when God is on our side. The story of Christ can be described as the story of God going to war in our behalf to conquer the enemy.

The passage in Ephesians that reads "he came and preached peace to you who were far off and peace to those who were near" is paraphrased by J. B. Phillips to read "then he came and told both you who were far from God and us who were near that the war was over" (Eph. 2:17).

We can lay hold on this vivid picture very concretely. During World War II no destruction touched the shores of America. Those who experienced the war were soldiers and civilians in faraway places. Yet we, too, were at war. Even untouched by immediate trouble, we felt its effects through rationing, worry over fathers and sons, anxiety about potential invasion, and related ways. Our whole life-style was geared to wartime. The very air we breathed and the ground we walked on were colored and tainted by the war.

The peace treaty was signed far away from our sight. We never heard the quiet of the cessation of shooting. Yet it brought as big a sigh of relief from us as it did from those directly involved. We went to the same homes and slept in our same beds, but we breathed differently, we felt something happen because peace had been declared. An event far removed from us changed everything about our life.

That is the picture of God's action in our behalf through Christ. What happened to and around and in Christ became a peace treaty as the forces that assaulted him had to surrender. They had met their match in Christ and sin could not overtake him nor could death hold him. They accomplished their worst by putting him to the cruel death on the cross and once they had done that they had nothing more to say. If he had a future beyond that, it was beyond their touch. And his resurrection announced his future. That is why Paul is bold to say things like: "For we know that Christ being raised from the dead will never die again; death no longer has dominion over him. The death he died he died to sin, once for all, but the life he lives he lives to God" (Rom. 6:9-10).

That is Paul's way of saying what Jesus says in the text. If Jesus has lived with and for God in such a way that sin could not destroy him in death, then anyone who has been embraced by him and lives under his lordship can dare to brave even death itself without fear. What cannot touch Christ cannot touch those who call themselves by his name, either. They have sheltered themselves in his victory, in other words. To live with him is to have the peace that is present in a life like his. The gracious gift of the Spirit of God in and through this Christ is the peace that comes from the Father's loving acceptance of us. Those whom the Spirit calls know well that the demonic spirit wars on and in and around them as it did over against Christ. But if it had to submit to Christ, so must it submit to those who commit their lives to his keeping. His peace treaty becomes ours. What was obtained by him is given to us.

So the enemy can rage all he wants. That which is most important for our lives is already done. Peace has been won and is offered by the Father through his Son as a gracious act of the Spirit as a free gift to those earnestly desiring it, seeking it, yearning for it.

Peace as an Aggressive Force

This peace has a peculiar power of its own, though. It is not a gift to be received and left sitting. That is the tie between the latter part of the text and the early part which reads: "He who has my commandments and keeps them, he it is who loves me; and he who loves me will be loved by my Father, and I will love him and manifest myself to him." God's peace had invaded the earth in this Christ who speaks, just as the Christmas angels had promised. God's peace aggressively moved toward people who needed it and longed for it. This peace comes wherever God sends his Spirit among men that he might testify to the possibilities of peace that have come anew to the earth in Christ.

And "love" is known where peace makes its presence felt. For "love" does not destroy, but builds up. It seeks to bring the peace of God among men so that harmony can be restored to a disordered world, so that people fragmented by fears may find wholeness and fulfillment again, so that relationships among people separated by sin may be restored.

This was the task to which the apostles were called, to lovingly proclaim and live the gospel of peace so that men and women everywhere might know the God of peace. One of those little known apostles whom we remember on this day, St. Jude (also called Thaddaeus), who is coupled in the tradition of the church with St. Simon the Zealot, is heard of only in connection with the question we hear him ask in our text aside from his simply being named as one of the twelve. Tradition says these two journeyed together (which is why the day celebrates the memory of both at the same time) to Persia where they were martyred on the same day.

They are the first wave, part of the larger host of witnesses to which you and I are called as the peace-makers on an earth where peace is hard to find. Save for these simple references mentioned, we know nothing of them. Nor will history know much of us here today . . . except for the fact that we, with them, continue the message of God's peace in lives committed to the love of God that drives us.

Should you wonder, by the way, about the two people whose story we spoke of in the beginning, I have no better answer than you may have had. God's peace can work in the midst of any life . . . whether it has much or has little, whether it suffers much or is virtually without physical and emotional torment. These are not the things that make for peace and thus pave the way for love.

The stories were only the framework for thought. The peace we asked about comes only from the Christ in whom the Father's love is revealed and poured out so that his peace might become our peace. When that peace rules in the life of a poor man, he is rich. And should the rich man not have that peace, he is poor. But it can and does enrich the lives of all who earnestly desire the gift, for Christ promises to give it freely. "Seek first his kingdom and his righteousness, and all these things shall be yours as well," Jesus said (Matt. 6:33).

To live with him as a citizen of his kingdom is to have his peace. And peace brings its own rewards.

HUBERT BECK
Texas A & M University
College Station, Texas

LUTHER NEVER CHANGED HIS NAME
Reformation Day
October 31
John 8:31-36

At one time in his life, Luther considered changing his name. There's a real freedom in that—selecting your own identity through the choice of an appropriate name. In Luther's day university scholars used to change their plain Swiss or German names into some Latin or Greek equivalent that would sound more elegant. For Luther the choice was particularly fitting, since the Greek word for "free" or "liberated" sounded very much like "Luther." By changing a letter or two, he could have taken that new name: "free."

There are few words left in our language that stimulate us as much as "free" or "freedom." Politicians know that an audience will always wake up when someone cries "Your freedom is threatened." Advertisers rely on the word "Free" in a headline to catch the casual buyer's eye. If you have ever played the game where people tell what animal they would like most to be, you remember that most folks choose animals that embody a sense of freedom. There must be something very deep within us that longs to feel free.

Yet there is also something deep within us that says we're not free *yet*. Young people join the army to free themselves from their past; they marry, sometimes, just to get away from home. You and I may have picked jobs that would make us independent. Yet we wake up sometime at about a quarter after forty and ask, "Where is that freedom I thought I was going to find? Where did it go? What happened to it?" Do we really have to wait, as the old spiritual says, until *death* before we can be "free at last"?

Born Free or Made Free?

Jesus addressed this constant human longing in the words recorded in John's Gospel, chapter eight. "If you dwell with the revelation I have brought you, you are indeed my disciples; you shall know the truth, and the truth shall make you free" (NEB). No wonder he drew crowds. Anyone who so reads the hunger within our hearts is assured of a hearing. Let's listen again carefully to those familiar words.

Did you notice where in the sentence the word "free" appeared? Not at the beginning, but at the end. Freedom is not where we start. It's the result of a series of actions. Jesus sketches them out: "dwell within the revelation I have brought," "be my disciples," "know the truth," and "the truth will make you free." We are not "born free"; we are "made free."

Just to say that we are not "born free," however, raises objections within us. We are certainly not born slaves; we live in a free country. We claim freedom as a right. In fact, the Declaration of Independence calls it an "inalienable right," a right that no one can take away. Who dares to say that we must be "made free" or "be liberated"?

If you have any tendency to react that way, then you can sympathize with those Jews who heard Jesus say these words in the temple. They responded, "We have never been in slavery to any man. What do you mean by saying, 'You will *become* free men' "? In that very objection, they proved that they were not free, because they did not know the truth about their own condition. If we were to recreate that scene on film today, we would start with our camera focused tightly on the little knot of people crowded around Jesus. As the discussion went on, we would draw back, taking in more of the surroundings, the courtyard, and the temple treasury. By the time the crowd was objecting "We have never been in slavery to any man" our camera would have risen to the point where it was taking in much of Jerusalem around the temple. There, clearly in the foreground would be the great Roman barracks where guards continually kept watch. They could look right down into the temple courtyard, seeing to it that no rebellion was being planned by their Jewish subjects. They need not have worried that day! Jesus' hearers had grown so accustomed to the Roman occupation that they boasted of their freedom—right under the eyes of their captors. How could they ever be freed until they admitted the truth?

The case is not much different with us. How can we ever be free until we know the cause of our captivity? True, there are no Roman garrisons in our city halls; we are politically free. But we don't *feel* free. We talk about the "walls closing in on us," about "decisions taken out of our hands," about being "powerless." What kind of slavery is this that has no bars, no chains, and no masters?

A Question of Identity

Jesus' words echo over the centuries, as if he had read our thoughts. "In very truth I tell you, everyone who commits sin is a slave."

At this point we must be very careful. It is so easy to launch into an attack on sin; but let's remember that our search is for truth, not only goodness. We are seeking freedom, and we must not be sidetracked by a false lead. Sin made its first captives in Eden, not by power, but by deceit. If we want to be free, we cannot be satisfied by trying to be good. We need to know the truth about ourselves.

"Know thyself" was a good motto. Socrates said it, and he tried to get his fellow citizens to practice it. But they found the effort at self-knowledge too tedious, so they put Socrates and his bothersome questions out of the way. Yet the fact that it is difficult to know ourselves as we really are may be the key to our whole search. If we can discover *why* it is futile to try to know ourselves, then we'll be on the way to a most important truth.

One of the mysteries of the Reformation is what sort of person Luther really was. One sixteenth-century tract calls him the "Apostle and Evangelist in the German Territories." Another tract calls him "a stinking bag of worms." Which was correct? Was Luther God's instrument, an "Apostle and Evangelist" of God's own truth? Or was he full of pride, lechery, and rebellion—no more than a "stinking bag of worms?" Before we dismiss this question as one of those unsolvable historical puzzles—since none of us was there or knew Luther personally—let me share an interesting fact with you. Those two conflicting estimates of Luther were not written by one-sided historians; they were both written by Luther himself.

Of course, to know that Luther's opinion of himself varied so widely just pushes the search for the real Luther back one more step. What sort of personality would call itself an "apostle" one time and a "bag of worms" another?

Or, put another way, why is it so hard for any of us to "see ourselves as others see us?" Like Luther, the more honestly we look at ourselves, the more conflicting evidence we find. We sometimes apologize, "I'm sorry, I'm just not myself today," yet we recognize that it was us, and not some outsider, who answered sharply or showed impatience. Which was the real "me"—the impatience or the apology?

Isn't that the real truth about ourselves—that we don't know our true selves? Or rather that our "true selves" change to suit the situation. And so we have no leverage, no point of departure from which we can assert our freedom. That's why we are so discontented. That's why we feel so "boxed in." It is not the world that has chained us, it is the lack of certainty within us. We are not caged; we are paralyzed.

One night I was traveling in my brother-in-law's boat along an unfamiliar coast. "Keep the bow pointed toward that light," he told me, and disappeared below. I did the best I could, peering through the darkness and trying to distinguish beacon lights from the lights of houses along the rocky shore. Suddenly my heart sank. The light I had been aiming toward was moving! It was not a landmark after all; it was simply the light of another ship's mast. I was lost in dangerous waters. In desperation I stopped the engine and waited there, adrift, until my brother-in-law could come up on deck and find our bearings.

The Reference Point

Freedom to act, then, requires a reliable reference point. We need some certainty outside ourselves. Jesus concludes his words with precisely that possibility: "If the Son sets you free, then you shall be free indeed." He said it earlier to the same group when he offered, "If you dwell within the revelation I have brought, you are indeed my disciples." Discipleship means finding a reference point in life. Then we know where we are. Our "world" makes sense.

That *external* reference point was Luther's secret of strength. He told how, as he lay awake at night, a little voice deep within him would say, "Do you think that all previous teachers were ignorant? Were all our fathers fools? Are you the only roost for the Holy Spirit in these last days?" Such thoughts froze his blood with dread. How could anyone with those inner doubts ever lead a Reformation?

Luther knew that his only hope for freedom from those dreads and doubts lay in keeping his eye fixed on Christ. He exploded when people started calling his followers "Lutherans." "What is Luther?" he cried. "The teaching is certainly not mine! I haven't been crucified for anybody! How could it then come to pass that Christ's children should be called by my name—poor stinking bag of worms that I am? I am no one's master, and I don't intend to be. I hold, along with everyone else, the common teaching of Jesus Christ, who alone is our master." Luther knew that his only hope lay in being a disciple. As long as Christ was his master, he would have the strength he needed. He could throw off the false values of his day and stand free.

We have discovered the reason why Luther never changed his name. He would not become free by his own declaration. He knew that it would never be in his own power to find freedom. He remained free only as long as he remained a disciple. So he prized the name that declared his allegiance: Christian.

You and I bear that name, too. A Reformation can happen within us. We can become free enough to change things in our family, our community, and our church. When "Christian" ceases to be a label, and becomes a life-style, freedom is possible at last.

HUGH GEORGE ANDERSON
Lutheran Theological Southern Seminary
Columbia, South Carolina

BLESSED ARE THOSE WHO MOURN

All Saints' Day
November 1
Matthew 5:1-12

Seeing the crowds, Jesus went up on the mountain . . . and taught them. Today we join them. With angels and archangels and with all the company of heaven, with the whole church militant and triumphant, we gather around the risen Lord. He opens his mouth and teaches us. His teaching repudiates and contradicts the teaching of the world. It turns everything upside down. The world says, get rich. Get rich quick. Jesus says, get poor. The world says, enjoy yourself, it's later than you think. Jesus says, blessed are those who mourn. The world says, have a drink. Eat hearty. Jesus says, hunger and thirst. The advertisements tell us to buy a lot of things. This will make you happy they say. Jesus says, happy are the poor. Go to the drugstore and you'll find a lot of things that will make you feel good, look good, smell good. The Bible talks about the whole creation groaning and travailing together. Quite a contradiction.

Blessed Are Those Who Mourn Their Dead

A mother in the Far East lost her only son. She was inconsolable. She went to the shrine and prayed to the lord Buddha that she might have her son back. Take a begging bowl, he said, and go to every house in the village. From every house where the family circle has not been broken by death, beg a peppercorn. When you come back at the end of the day with your bowl full, you will have your son back.

The woman rejoiced. She set out on her way. At the end of the day she returned without one single peppercorn in her bowl. Blessed are those who mourn, Jesus says. There is not one of us here today who does not grieve over someone whom we have loved and lost awhile. There is not one family circle represented before this altar today which has not been broken by death.

We remember our blessed dead especially at this time and at this service. Mourning means to face the fact as Christians that death is not simply a process of nature but that it indeed is the wages of sin and the last enemy to be destroyed. Yet we spend billions of dollars trying to cover it up and pretend that it isn't so terrible after all. We cover it with cosmetics and flowers and fancy coffins, and all the time Jesus is saying, blessed are those who mourn. Mourning means to realize—to make real—the fact of physical death. Mourning means to realize—to make real— that there is only one thing worse: spiritual death. Jesus teaches us not to be afraid of those who kill the body but cannot kill the soul; rather be afraid of God who can destroy both body and soul in hell (Matt. 10:28).

Blessed are those who see death for what it is, for they shall be comforted. Not mollycoddled. Not lulled into any false optimism. But *strengthened*. Blessed are those who mourn, for they shall be strengthened. Strengthened by the remembrance that Jesus, True Man, himself died, that he was buried and that on the third day he rose again from the dead and lives and reigns to all eternity. The comfort, the strength that all of us have today as we remember our dear ones who have gone before us with the sign of faith is Christ the victor. Thanks be to God who gives us the victory through our Lord Jesus Christ. We are one in him and with those we love in the mystical sweet communion of the company of saints.

Blessed Are Those Who Mourn the Way the World Is

Our word *mourn* is too much limited to the funeral parlor. We need to stretch it a little. Blessed are those who mourn for sin and pain in the world. Blessed are those who mourn. It is the most perplexing of all the beatitudes. We're supposed to *mourn?* What about all the times we have heard that as Christians we're supposed to rejoice and be glad? How often do you see a snapshot of scowling, mournful people? No. Most of the time they have been told to smile and say something idiotic. So on their faces is a superficial, empty grin. A lot of people face life that way—with an empty smile. When Jesus says "mourn," it means we are to face up to reality. Not only in death, not only when we lose someone dear to us. "There are tears in things," Vergil wrote. Life is often hard, tragic, inexplicable.

> He that lacks time to mourn, lacks time to mend.
> Eternity mourns that. 'Tis an ill cure
> For life's worst ills, to have no time to feel them.
> Where sorrow's held intrusive and turned out
> There wisdom will not enter, nor true power,
> Nor aught that dignifies humanity.

Blessed are those who mourn for sin and pain. It was not the Israelites who accepted captivity with an empty smile, it was not those who were absorbed by their pagan captors who were the blessed ones. It was the remnant who mourned. It was the few who sat down and wept by the waters of Babylon, who could not—even though they were commanded—who could not sing the Lord's song in a strange land. The blessed ones, the saints, were those like Daniel who kept his window open toward Jerusalem, his hope anchored there and his prayers flying up to the living God. They were the saints, the blessed ones, who were strengthened and comforted to endure the long captivity, the weary journey back and the grim and backbreaking task of rebuilding the windswept ruins of the Holy City.

We can go through life with the superficial smile of the 20th century which proclaims, "I'm OK; You're OK," which broadcasts the idea that there is really no such thing as sin. That is really to be a present-day captive in Babylon. But if you want to be counted among the company of the blessed ones, the holy ones, the saints in Jesus Christ, it means to mourn, it means to have our eyes wide open to our own sin—how I fall short of doing God's will for me—how I fail to help my neighbor in need. Mourning means to realize—to make real—the sinfulness of the whole world of man.

> The Lord looks down from
> heaven at mankind
> to see if there are any who are wise,
> any who worship him.
> But they have all gone wrong;
> they are all equally bad.
> Not one of them does right,
> not a single one. (Ps. 14 TEV)

Mourning means to open our eyes to the tragedies of war, starvation, sickness and man's inhumanity to man. It means to be aware of man's cruelty and unheeding exploitation of nature. "Once there was a church that prayed for their nation and for peace and the president at the end of the hour. Many people got restless because the prayers seemed long. Now they have a television set in their church and they all pray when the news is on. There's one man who turns on the news very clearly, so everyone can see it. All the people say the words: Hear us and help us good Lord. They do it during the whole news broadcast. Even the ads" (Herbert Brokering: *I Openers*) That's mourning. It's being conscious of the way it really should be and the way it is. The evil conditions of the earth, though widely tolerated, are intolerable to a saint. If you see God's family as your family, no human cross will be of indifference to you.

For those who have never heard of the love of God—those who ignore or reject the tears in things—they couldn't care less and their life turns into cynicism and despair. If you don't care, you can certainly avoid mourning. It is when you look at what is in the world and mourn for the way it might have been that you fulfill your sainthood and so are blessed. It is when you look at your own life and mourn for what you might have been that you are a saint. The beatitudes are spoken to saints. It is only when we face squarely and honestly the ravages of sin, death and pain that comfort is assured.

Today with ten thousand times ten thousand of the saints in light we gather around the risen and ascended Lord. He contradicts and turns upside down the ideas of the world. Blessed are those who mourn, he tells us. Blessed are those who know the grief and separation of death, for they shall be comforted. Blessed are those who have their eyes open to the suffering, pain and evil in the world, for they shall be comforted. Their strength and fortitude shall come from the crucified and Risen One who reigns from the cross and tells us, "Fear not, I have overcome the world."

It's called All Saints' Day. That means it's your day too.

CHARLES TREXLER
Lutheran Church of the Good Shepherd
Roosevelt, New York